28 GREAT
AMERICAN CITIES
BED &
BREAKFAST
GUIDE

A Handel lamp at Evelo's Bed & Breakfast, Minneapolis.

Afternoon tea at A CAMBRIDGE HOUSE *in Cambridge, Mass., outside of Boston.*

28 GREAT AMERICAN CITIES

Bed & Breakfast Guide

BY TERRY BERGER, ROBERT REID,
LUCY POSHEK, AVERY AND SUE PITZAK,
AND KATHERINE JOHNSTON

Photographs by Lucy Poshek, et al

DESIGNED AND PRODUCED BY
ROBERT R. REID AND TERRY BERGER

PRENTICE HALL TRAVEL

NEW YORK   LONDON   TORONTO   SYDNEY   TOKYO   SINGAPORE

FRONT COVER: Southmoreland On the Plaza, Kansas City, Missouri.

Published by Prentice Hall General Reference
15 Columbus Circle
New York, NY 10023-7780

PRENTICE HALL is a registered trademark
and Colophon is a trademark of Prentice-Hall Inc.

ISBN 0-671-88035-7

Library of Congress catalog card no: 93-87439

A Robert Reid Associates production
Typeset in Bodoni Book by Monotype Composition Company, Baltimore
Produced by Mandarin Offset, Hong Kong
Printed in Hong Kong

1 2 3 4 5 6 7 8 9 10

CONTENTS

ATLANTA
8 Beverly Hills Inn
10 Shellmont Bed and Breakfast Lodge
11 The Woodruff Bed & Breakfast Inn
12 Ansley Inn

BALTIMORE
14 The Admiral Fell Inn
15 Betsy's Bed & Breakfast
15 The Shirley Madison Inn
16 Society Hill Hopkins
17 Green Spring Valley

BOSTON
18 A Cambridge House
20 Beacon Hill
20 Copley Square
21 On the Avenue
22 The Terrace Townehouse

CHARLESTON
23 Villa de la Fontaine
24 Two Meeting Street Inn
26 The John Rutledge House Inn
27 Vendue Inn
28 Maison Dupré

CHICAGO
29 Lincoln Park
30 City View Inn
31 Cheney House

DALLAS / FORT WORTH
32 The Stockyards Hotel
33 Miss Molly's Hotel
34 Hotel St. Germain

DENVER
36 Castle Marne
38 Queen Anne Inn
39 Haus Berlin
40 Merritt House
40 Many Mansions

KANSAS CITY
41 WynBrick Inn Bed & Breakfast
42 Southmoreland on the Plaza
44 Doanleigh Wallagh Inn

LOS ANGELES
46 Salisbury House Bed & Breakfast
48 La Maida House & Bungalows
49 Venice Beach House
50 The Inn at 657
50 Lord Mayor's Inn Bed & Breakfast
51 Channel Road Inn

MIAMI
52 Colony Hotel
54 Biscayne Bay
54 Coconut Grove
55 Horse Country
56 Hotel Place St. Michel

MINNEAPOLIS / ST. PAUL
58 Chatsworth Bed & Breakfast
60 1900 Dupont
61 Evelo's Bed & Breakfast
62 LeBlanc House

NEW ORLEANS
64 The Josephine Guest House
66 Lamothe House
67 Lafitte Guest House
68 Soniat House

NEW YORK
69 Inn New York City
70 Gramercy Park
71 Greenwich Village
71 Upper West Side
72 Sutton Place
72 Gracie Mansion Area
73 Upper East Side

PHILADELPHIA
74 La Reserve
75 The Thomas Bond House
76 The Independence Park Inn
77 Shippen Way Inn

PHOENIX / SCOTTSDALE
78 Westways Resort B & B Inn
79 Inn at the Citadel
80 Scottsdale B&B
82 Maricopa Manor

PORTLAND
83 Heron Haus Bed & Breakfast Inn
84 White House
85 MacMaster House

ST. LOUIS
86 The Winter House
87 The Eastlake Inn Bed & Breakfast
88 The Antique Shop Bed & Breakfast
88 Lafayette House

SALT LAKE CITY
89 Saltair Bed and Breakfast
90 Pine Crest Bed & Breakfast Inn
92 Brigham Street Inn

continued overleaf

SAN ANTONIO
94   The Ogé House
96   Falling Pines B&B Inn
97   Beckmann Inn and Carriage House
98   Terrell Castle Bed and Breakfast

SAN DIEGO
99   Heritage Park Bed & Breakfast Inn
100   Dockside Inn
102   Keating House

SAN FRANCISCO
103   Victorian Inn on the Park
104   Washington Square Inn
106   Alamo Square Inn
106   The Bed and Breakfast Inn
107   Spencer House
108   The Archbishop's Mansion

SANTA FE
109   Alexander's Inn
110   Grant Corner Inn
111   Dos Casas Viejas
112   El Paradero

SEATTLE
113   Gaslight Inn
114   M.V. Challenger
116   The Beech Tree Manor
116   Chambered Nautilus
117   Roberta's

TUCSON
118   La Posada del Valle Bed & Breakfast Inn
120   El Presidio Bed & Breakfast Inn
121   Rimrock West
122   Peppertrees B&B Inn

WASHINGTON, D.C.
123   The Kalorama Guest House
124   Morrison-Clark
126   Logan Circle
127   BED & BREAKFAST AGENCIES

ATLANTA

BEVERLY HILLS INN

European-style bed and breakfast

All bed and breakfasts have an individual character that distinguishes them from each other. The Beverly Hills Inn, for example, features itself as a European style hotel which is small and intimate, with just seventeen rooms and suites, individually decorated with period furnishings, private baths, telephones, and color television.

Such a billing is obviously attractive, because twenty-five per cent of the clientele is European, including foreign diplomats and overseas visitors put up there by local banks.

The small, fine hotel ambience emanates from the hotel's owner, Mit Amin, himself an internationalist from the north of England. He feels perfectly at home in Atlanta's affluent Buckhead neighborhood, where the inn is located, with its tree-lined streets and hand-hewn stone houses similar to the England he knows and remembers so fondly.

Located just off Peachtree Street, Atlanta's most famous thoroughfare, it is easy to find your way straight into downtown Atlanta, fifteen minutes away, or to any number of other nearby attractions. These include two sensational shopping malls—Lenox and Phipps Plaza—featuring Neiman-Marcus, Lord & Taylor, Saks Fifth Avenue, Macy's, and Rich's.

A sitting room.

BEVERLY HILLS INN, 65 Sheridan Drive N.E., Atlanta, GA 30305; (404) 233-8520; Mit Amin, owner. Open all year. Eighteen rooms, all with private baths. Rates: per room, from $74 to $120 for suites, including a continental-plus breakfast. Children welcome; pets welcome; smoking permitted; Visa/MasterCard/American Express/Discover/Diners/JCB.

DIRECTIONS: from downtown, go north on Peachtree to Sheridan. Inn is one-half block down.

The exquisitely restored house.

SHELLMONT

A perfect restoration

Decorated like a piece of Wedgewood china, this lovely 1891 shell-motif Victorian was built by one of Atlanta's important architects, W.T. Downing. Commissioned by a prominent doctor, whose portrait still hangs in the foyer, the Atlanta landmark has been lovingly restored by restoration-owner Ed McCord and his wife Debbie, who have left bits of wall and ceiling exposed in some rooms to display the original décor.

Two turn-of-the-century parlors, with lace-covered windows, piano-tile fireplaces, kilim rugs, and pillow-strewn sofas, and a library decked out as a Turkish corner, provide generous lounging areas. The second floor foyer has a direct view of the beautiful stained-glass windows that are thought to be early Tiffany.

Three guest rooms, a Green room, a Blue room, and a Rose room, have been brought back to their original color and stenciled borders, and furnished with Eastlake and Victorian pieces. A fully equipped carriage house in the rear has a turn-of-the-century ambience and twentieth-century comforts. Front and back porches have hanging pots of blooms and wicker rockers.

Breakfast cereal, fruit, croissants, European tarts, or strudel are set out on the sideboard of the dining room, alive with potted palms. The affable hosts, who know and love every inch of this house, succeed in making this bed and breakfast experience a very personal one.

SHELLMONT BED AND BREAKFAST LODGE, 821 Piedmont Avenue N.E., Atlanta, GA 30308; (404) 872-9290; Ed and Debbie McCord, owners. Open all year. Four guest rooms (1 in carriage house) with private baths. Rates: $67 single, $77 double (carriage house $87 single, $97 double), including continental breakfast. Children over 12 in carriage house only; no pets; limited smoking; Visa/MasterCard/American Express. Restaurants in area include The Abbey, the Pleasant Peasant for continental, and Ciboulette for French cuisine.

DIRECTIONS: call for explicit instructions, depending on where you are.

The ornately detailed entry hall.

An attractively decorated sideboard.

A Guest room.

THE WOODRUFF B&B INN

Spirited restoration

The dominating theme of the Woodruff Inn is Bessie Woodruff herself, a colorful former owner of the inn who ran it as a massage parlor. That's Bessie on the inn's brochure, and the mantel is lined with photographs of her.

By 1989, four years after Bessie's death, the building, run down by then, was acquired by Doug Jones, his cousin Dan, and their wives, Joan and Sandy. It should be explained that Doug has "old house disease." Whenever he sees a weathered old house, he gets the overwhelming desire to buy it and fix it up.

Today, the inn is indeed "fixed up." Twelve attractive guest rooms, varying from Victorian to turn-of-the-century to 1920s decor, welcome guests in a variety of accommodations—deluxe suites, single rooms, and family suites, all with private baths. In addition, guests have a choice of full southern or continental breakfasts, either served in their room or in the main dining room.

Conveniently situated in the heart of Atlanta, the inn has a superb variety of restaurants within one block. These include Mary Mac's Tea Room, one of the best restaurants in the country; The Crab House, famous for its seafood; The Mansion, noted for its Victorian architecture and fine cuisine; and The Abbey, holder of the most awards for fine dining in Atlanta.

THE WOODRUFF BED & BREAKFAST INN, 223 Ponce de Leon Avenue, Atlanta, GA 30308; (404) 875-9449; Joan and Douglas Jones, owners. Open all year. Twelve rooms, 6 with private baths, 6 share 3 adjoining baths; 2 suites have hot tubs. Rates: $65 to $99 single, $75 to $125 double, including full southern breakfast. Children welcome; no pets; smoking limited; Spanish spoken; Visa/MasterCard/Discover. Great dining 1 block away.

DIRECTIONS: from Peachtree, turn east on Ponce de Leon for 3 blocks. (Watch for the famous Fox Theater, that premiered *Gone With the Wind*, at the corner of Peachtree and Ponce de Leon.)

ANSLEY INN

Atlanta's charms

This is the story of a beautiful old turn-of-the-century Tudor mansion in a chic residential area of Atlanta that was left to deteriorate into a local eyesore. Since it was too fine a house to tear down, the neighbors instead meticulously restored it and turned it into a luxurious bed and breakfast inn with a 24-hour concierge service and a lavish breakfast buffet that gets you going in the morning.

Details include massive fireplaces, crystal chandeliers, Oriental rugs, and Chippendale, Queen Anne, and Empire furniture.

Amenities in each guest room include cable television, private telephones, private baths with Jacuzzis, a wet bar, individual climate control, and breakfast in your own room if you prefer. Throughout the house there is a revolving exhibition of paintings and drawings, all of which are for sale.

Conveniences include a health club with state-of-the-art exercise equipment, a steam bath, and

tanning facilities. Atlanta's High Museum, Woodruff Art Center, and Botanical Gardens are right in the neighborhood.

ANSLEY INN, 253 Fifteenth Street, Atlanta, GA 30309; (800) 446-5416; (404) 872-9000; Tim Thomas, manager. Open all year. Fifteen guest rooms with private baths. Rates: $100 to $250 per room, including buffet continental breakfast and afternoon tea. Well-supervised children welcome; pets welcome; Visa/MasterCard/American Express/En Route; translation service available.

DIRECTIONS: from I-75 or I-85 exit at Fourteenth Street and go east to Peachtree Street. Turn left for 1 block to Fifteenth Street and bear right to inn on right.

BALTIMORE

A typical spacious, high-ceilinged guest room.

THE ADMIRAL FELL INN

Waterfront luxury lodgings

Fell's Point is Baltimore's most authentic waterfront neighborhood. The central focus is the 208-year-old market square, which borders on the harbor where clipper ships used to dock. A stone's throw from the harbor, dominating the Square and the market buildings, sits the four-story Admiral Fell, a combination of three different, contiguous brick buildings that functioned as a seafarers' boarding house, a bottling plant, and a private house.

Beautifully restored, the inn contains 37 guest rooms, all furnished differently, with fine period reproductions which contribute to the overall ambience of elegant Georgian interiors. Each guest room is named for someone of local prominence, an example of which is the blue-carpeted Robert Oliver Room, named after an Irish merchant who became one of Baltimore's early millionaires. Yellow walls with floral borders and two four poster beds with snowy white bedspreads and lace canopies decorate the spacious room.

A number of guest rooms (those with a number ending in 03) look out on the square and the pier where the boats dock.

The inn is a stone's throw from the Fell's Point boat dock.

Fell's Point originally was a bustling village of shipyards, warehouses, canneries, and private homes of sea captains and sailors for 150 years. Most activity ground to a halt during the Great Depression of the 1930s, and the whole area lay fallow until twenty years ago, suffering only from benign neglect, rather than the total destruction visited upon a lot of neighborhoods in the name of development.

Today we can enjoy a restored eighteenth-century village of town houses, pubs, boutiques, art galleries, restaurants, junk shops, market stalls that all blend together to make Fell's Point a unique part of Baltimore.

THE ADMIRAL FELL INN, 888 South Broadway, Baltimore, MD 21231; (800) 292-4667; Dominik Echenstein, innkeeper. Open all year. 37 guest rooms with private baths, 3 with Jacuzzis. Rates: $110 to $145 per room, including continental breakfast. Children welcome; no pets; non-smoking rooms available; wheelchair accessible; all major credit cards. Complimentary van drop-off service to Camden Yards ball park, Harborplace, and other downtown locations. Water taxi from jetty at foot of Market Sq. to Harborplace and Little Italy. Inn has its own gourmet restaurant or there is Bertha's, famous for seafood, a block away. The most famous extravaganza of all is Hausner's for Chesapeake seafood.

DIRECTIONS: ask when you make reservations.

BETSY'S BED & BREAKFAST

Historic Baltimore

A four-story brick row house in the historic Bolton Hill district affords guests a wonderful opportunity to experience the elegant grandeur of the post Civil War life of Baltimore's more affluent citizens. Notables like Gertrude Stein, F. Scott Fitzgerald, and the Cone sisters lived in the neighborhood.

High ceilings, floors of alternating strips of oak and walnut, carved marble mantels, and a center staircase rising four stories to a rooftop skylight give some idea of the architectural details that delight the eye.

At the rear of the house, a deck and hot tub shaded by a large oak tree afford the physical ease and relaxation that one also looks for in a good bed and breakfast. King and queen-sized beds in all the guest rooms contribute to the generally relaxed atmosphere. Top it all off with a delicious breakfast, and your stay is complete.

BETSY'S BED & BREAKFAST. Three guest rooms with private baths. Open all year. Rates: $75 double, including full breakfast. Children welcome; no pets; no smoking. Near Inner Harbor, which is noted for fine dining. *Represented by Amanda's Regional Service for Bed & Breakfast*, 1428 Park Avenue, Baltimore, MD 21217; (800) 899-7533; Fax (410) 728-8957; Betsy Grater. Visa/MasterCard/American Express/Discover.

DIRECTIONS: given on reservation.

The common room, where guests meet for coffee.

THE SHIRLEY MADISON INN

A period-style hotel

A true in-town lodging, The Shirley Madison has period style without being prissy or pretentious, and is a comfortable place in which to experience turn-of-the-century living. The Park Court is a sister lodging which adjoins the main building across a common courtyard that is set up with tables during nice weather.

Charming stone carvings and marble pillars complement the red-brick façade of the 110-year-old main building. Inside, common rooms and a beautifully-papered parlor flank a winding oak staircase leading up to guest rooms. The rooms, all individually appointed, are furnished with an interesting assortment of Victorian and Edwardian antiques, and an equal measure of comfort. The small, vintage open-grille elevator offers an alternative to climbing the stairs.

A continental breakfast is presented buffet-style, and the hosts are friendly and helpful, often beyond duty—even an absent guest's dog may be taken out for a walk.

The inn is located in the historic Mount Vernon section, near Baltimore's elegant Washington Monument, and only minutes from the Walters Art Gallery.

THE SHIRLEY MADISON INN, 205 West Madison Street, Baltimore, MD 21201; (410) 728-6550, (800) 868-5064; John Jorgenson and Mike Mullor, managers. Open all year. Twenty-five rooms with private baths, 12 with kitchenettes, 4 with parlors. Rates: $85 to $105 single or double, including continental buffet breakfast, evening sherry, tea and coffee all day. Children welcome (under 12 free); small pets welcome; 3 smoking floors, 1 non-smoking floor; Visa/MasterCard/American Express/Diners Club. Parking on premises. Near North Charles Street restaurants, shops, and galleries.

DIRECTIONS: west of Washington Monument off Charles St. N.

The richness and warmth of the parlor.

SOCIETY HILL HOPKINS

Four periods to choose from

The first room you notice is the charming parlor with its floral couch and matching wallpaper border, faux-finish mantel, etched-glass Victorian chandelier, handsome artworks, and lace panel curtains. Guests often relax here with a cup of coffee or a glass of wine.

The twenty-six guest rooms in this Spanish revival building have been arranged into four different periods: Federal, Victorian, Art Deco, and Contemporary. Guests are invited to reserve that period room that suits their mood or sense of fantasy.

Gray, lavender, peach, and blue offset the patterned rugs in the Federal room. The wallpaper border is a classical Adams frieze, and the mahogany armoire, Chippendale-style chairs, draped valances, and old prints enhance the period effect.

The Victorian room features a dressing mirror, wicker desk, white iron sweetheart bedstead, marble-topped tables, and lace curtains, while the Art Deco room has black lacquer furniture, Chinese-style lamps, twenties prints, and touches of period maroons and greys.

Finally, the contemporary room in browns and persimmon, accented in green, has a bed with brass headboard, rattan night stands, a pine armoire, and Hitchcock-style chair.

The monotony of the usual assemblage of small hotel rooms will not be found here; appointments do not smack of the decorator's art. Instead the charm of European bed and breakfasts and the warm hospitality of American country inns combines in a uniquely exciting blend.

SOCIETY HILL HOPKINS, 3404 St. Paul Street, Baltimore, MD 21218; (410) 235-8600; Ken Scheuering, innkeeper. A historic building in a historic neighborhood. Open all year. Twenty-six guest rooms, including suites, all with private baths; some with kitchenettes. Rates: $70–$135. Continental breakfast. Children welcome; no pets; smoking permitted; major credit cards accepted. Within walking distance of Baltimore Museum of Art, one block from Johns Hopkins University.

DIRECTIONS: call for directions.

Truly a mansion.

GREEN SPRING VALLEY

A Cassatt family estate

Steeped in history, this secluded 26-room majestic estate, situated on 45 acres of Maryland's splendid Green Spring Valley, is just twenty minutes from Baltimore's Inner Harbor. Bed and breakfast is savored amidst the elegance enjoyed at the turn of the century.

It was built as a wedding gift for his daughter by Alexander J. Cassatt, president of the Pennsylvania Railroad and brother of Mary Cassatt, the impressionist painter. Later it became the home to descendants of Benjamin Franklin, and still later, the site of the Koinonia Foundation, a precursor of the Peace Corps, that trained people in literacy methods and organic gardening for service on every continent.

The house became a bed and breakfast shortly after it was purchased in 1985, and was furnished with choice antiques, beautiful artworks, and authentic period furniture. The baronial first floor has recessed paneling, beamed ceilings, huge fireplaces, a grand piano, oriental carpets, and that all-too-fast disappearing treasure, a library.

There are four elegant guest rooms: Aphrodite's Retreat, in shades of pink and mauve, sun-dappled and bedecked with French antiques; Aunt Mary's Suite, splendid in Victorian trappings with a canopied bed, fireplace, and claw-footed tub; the Ambassador's Room, a romantic guest room with intricate blue and gold wallpaper, fireplace, Jacuzzi, and elegant statuary shower; the Blue Garden Suite, a beautiful three-room suite with Louis XIV furniture, fireplace, and sun porch overlooking the olympic-sized pool.

Guests are welcome to swim in the pool, enjoy the hot tub, play tennis, visit the orchard, and the shitake mushroom plantings and herb gardens.

A gourmet breakfast served on fine china on the porch or by the fireplace in the dining room, depending on the season, features blackberries year round, a mushroom, tomato, and onion herb omelet, berry pancakes, and a vegetable dish delicacy.

In addition to all of the aforementioned bounty, this wonderful place and its engaging hosts are child friendly.

GREEN SPRING VALLEY. Four guest rooms with private baths. Open all year. Rates: $90 to $125 double, including full breakfast. Children welcome; no pets; no smoking. Good dining in area. *Represented by Amanda's Regional Reservation Service for Bed & Breakfast,* 1428 Park Avenue, Baltimore, MD 21217; (800) 899-7533; Fax (410) 728-8957; Betsy Grater. Visa/MasterCard/American Express/Discover.
DIRECTIONS: given on reservation.

The guest rooms are individually and extravagantly decorated.

BOSTON

A CAMBRIDGE HOUSE

A fantasy of fabrics

Even the BBC has taken note of A Cambridge House, heralding it as "Boston's premier bed and breakfast." And no wonder!

Built in 1892, the Colonial Revival house is decorated with a flourish—with rolls of Victorian wallpapers and bolts of Waverly fabrics, oriental carpets, antique furniture, heavy draperies, and Chinese export bric-a-brac—looking very much the *Grande Dame* of Victoriana.

Through three owners the house has maintained its original integrity. Six working fireplaces, built-in corner cabinets, and beautiful hardwood floors are all original to the house. Owners Ellen Riley and Anthony Femmino bought the nine bedroom house as a residence, but after a few discerning guests were permitted to stay, a bed and breakfast was born.

Boston designers Dottie Scully and Tish Stagnone festooned the rooms with dainty floral and ribbon patterns, lavished with hundreds of yards of Waverly chintzes, damasks, and jacquards. Canopies, dust ruffles, swag curtains, and fresh floral bouquets create a romantic mood that resonates from room to room.

Breakfast is served in the parlor that connects to a luxurious den—and what a treat awaits you! A full breakfast is prepared by a talented chef, and may include delicate quiches, tasty omelets, fruit-topped waffles, and specially prepared low-fat sausage. All manner of complimentary goodies are available throughout the day.

A CAMBRIDGE HOUSE. 2218 Massachusetts Avenue, Cambridge, MA 02140-1836; (800) 232-9989, (617) 491-6300, FAX (617) 868-2848; Ellen Riley, Anthony Femmino, owners. Open all year. Nine guest rooms with private baths in main house, 5 rooms sharing baths in carriage house. Rates: *main house* $89 to $185; *carriage house* $85 to $159, including chef-prepared full breakfast and special breakfast on Sundays. Inquire about children; no pets; no smoking; Visa/MasterCard/American Express. Many fine restaurants nearby.

DIRECTIONS: Massachusetts Avenue is a main thoroughfare running from Boston to Cambridge.

A breakfast to remember.

KIMBERLY GRANT PHOTOGRAPH

BEACON HILL

Stately guest rooms

Located on Boston's prestigious Beacon Hill and adjacent to the Massachusetts State House, the inn consists of two attached 1830s brick townhouses of twenty stately guest rooms. It is perfectly located for visiting the Boston Common, the Public Gardens, the Freedom Trail, and the Faneuil Hall/Quincy Market district.

The inn has been entirely renovated and charmingly decorated with beautiful period furnishings, and many guest rooms feature four-poster and canopied beds, decorative fireplaces, desks, private baths, and air conditioning. The rooms are striking, with floral patterns covering the walls and coordinated bed spreads and draperies complementing the tall windows that look out on the city.

An open kitchen is provided for self-serve breakfasts, and guests are always welcome to use the kitchen, the dining room, and the attractive parlors.

BEACON HILL. Attached 1830s brick townhouses with 20 guest rooms, 18 of which have private baths; there are 4 meeting rooms for conferences. Open all year. Rates: $80 single, $90 double, $15 additional guests. Includes stocked kitchen where you prepare your own full breakfast. Children welcome; no pets; no smoking; agency accepts all credit cards. Directions on reservation. *Represented by Bed and Breakfast Associates, Bay Colony Ltd., Boston, MA. (617) 449-5302.*

COPLEY SQUARE

A culinary treat

This restored 1863 five-story brick townhouse is set in the historic district adjacent to Boston's renowned Copley Square. It is within strolling distance of elegant restaurants, outdoor cafés, nearby theaters, the Hynes Convention Center, and bus and subway lines.

Sensitive attention to detail and gracious hospitality are the hallmark of this bed and breakfast. Each impeccable guest room offers uniquely decorative features including wide pine floors, bow windows, marble fireplaces, brass beds, armoires, full length paisley draperies, Chinese rugs, queen sized beds, and private baths. For those who would like them, four of the rooms provide a discreet galley kitchenette.

A generous full breakfast is served in the sunfilled penthouse breakfast room that is alive with skylights and views of the city. The host's culinary skills are showcased when he prepares and serves his perfectly turned blueberry buttermilk pancakes, French toast with tangy strawberry sauce, or old-fashioned scrambled eggs with succulent sausage. Those who prefer privacy are invited to enjoy a continental breakfast in their room.

COPLEY SQUARE. 1863 brick townhouse with 3 guest rooms with private baths. Open all year. Rates: $97 double, including full breakfast. Older children welcome; no pets; no smoking; agency accepts all credit cards. Directions on reservation. *Represented by Bed and Breakfast Associates, Bay Colony, Ltd., Boston, MA. (617) 449-5302.*

FAY FOTO

In the heart of Boston's Back Bay

A Victorian townhouse located in Boston's historic Back Bay is the home of a private club that offers its classic hospitality and quiet sophistication to selected guests through the Host Homes of Boston reservation service.

Steeped in history, the club has offered cultural and intellectual programs since 1890. Before that, it was the private home of the Robbins family, famous Boston clock makers.

The high-ceilinged guest rooms are attractively decorated with period antiques. The rooms with fireplaces also have private baths, whereas the other rooms share a bath for each two rooms. Breakfast is served in the formal dining room.

Within walking distance are the theater district, Beacon Hill, the Public Garden, Copley Place, Boston Common, and the smart boutiques, cafés, and galleries of Newberry Street, where Boston's elite like to meet.

ON THE AVENUE. Open all year. 4 doubles with twin beds and private baths; 5 singles, each sharing a bath with one other room. Rates: $60 to $90 single, $105 double; rollaways $25; including continental breakfast. Children 10 and over welcome; no pets; smoking in drawing room; Hungarian spoken; Visa/MasterCard/American Express. *Represented by Host Homes of Boston*, P.O. Box 117, Waban Branch, Boston, MA 02168; (617) 244-1308; Marcia Whittington.

DIRECTIONS: Maps mailed with confirmation. Some parking available.

FAY FOTO

A new addition is the Rooftop Garden, where breakfast can be enjoyed amidst birch trees, cosmos, roses, and poppies.

THE TERRACE TOWNEHOUSE

A dedicated preservationist

Two blocks from Copley Place, and a short stroll from the Public Garden and Newberry Street, The Terrace Townehouse thrives under the stewardship of a dedicated and knowledgeable host. Gloria Belknap's touch is revealed in everything—from the Victorian floral arrangements and wall-hung decorative plates, to the Brie omelets, German pancakes, and cheese blintzes she mastered in Paris while studying at La Varenne.

Four charming guest rooms offer the visitors a variety of fantasies. The Bay-windowed British Officer's Room has a half-tester bedstead and ephemera of a bygone romantic era. The China Trade Room is awash in bright yellow, with a sea-captain's trunk, framed Chinese wedding skirt, and a panel from a Chinese wedding bed.

Breakfasts are served in the privacy of the guest rooms with crystal and china. A charming backdrop for afternoon tea, the third-floor library, with its floral easy chairs and needlepoint carpet, offers books for browsing, chess, and board games.

Exhuberant Ms. Belknap enjoys sharing her beloved home and her love for the past. "To maintain an antique," she states, "is to preserve our heritage."

THE TERRACE TOWNEHOUSE. 60 Chandler St., Boston, MA 02116; (617) 350-6520; Gloria Belknap, owner. Open all year. Four guest rooms with private baths. Rates; $115 to $140 per room, including full breakfast served in room (off-season rates available). No children; no pets; no smoking; Portuguese and a little French and Spanish spoken; Visa/MasterCard.

DIRECTIONS: walking distance from Back Bay Amtrak station and 2½ blocks from Copley Place shopping mall. Local nearby landmark is I.M. Pei's Hancock Tower.

CHARLESTON

The stunning stairway to the 2nd floor.

VILLA DE LA FONTAINE

A Mecca for antiques lovers

Having worked for the Guggenheims, Chases, and Fleischmans, during the furnishing of their great homes and plantations, Bill Fontaine and his partner Aubrey Hancock, entertain museum bigwigs with élan. All arriving guests are treated similarly—an hour-long tour through rooms that are furnished with objects that rival and sometimes surpass those displayed at the Metropolitan Museum of Art, Winterthur, and the Smithsonian.

Highlights of the tour include a verdi-marble table by William Kent, who designed Hampton Court, a bronze torchiére that burns perfumed oil, Scalamandré fabrics, highboys of rare and exquisite woods and craftsmanship, a unique heart-pine South

Carolina bookcase, Meissen, Wedgewood, a glorious verdi-and-rouge-marble fireplace, and miniature ivory portraits. The latter were recently included in a stunning exhibit at Charleston's Gibbes Museum of Art. Heirlooms that belonged to the most notable Southern families abound here, in these fourteen-foot-ceilinged rooms in this incredible Greek temple of a building.

Notice the 1810 French ice cream urns in the drawing room—a status symbol for wealthy Southerners when ice had to be delivered from the North and stored underground to be used to make ice cream for those few who could afford it.

Breakfast is in the solarium, a bright, colorful room with fan windows and a delightful hand-painted mural. Waffles, sausage, eggs Benedict, hashed browns, hot spiced fruit or compôte are served, and the tangy marmalade is made from fruit trees in the garden.

There is a lovely, spacious garden and piazza, with two houses for the thirty-four slaves that it took to run the house. All those jobs have been taken over by Bill and Aubrey, two knowledgeable, hard working, and gracious hosts.

VILLA DE LA FONTAINE, 138 Wentworth Street, Charleston, SC 29401; (803) 577-7709; William Fontaine and Aubrey Hancock, owners and innkeepers. Open all year; 4 guest accommodations, with exotic full breakfast. Rates: $100 to $165 per room. Children not encouraged; no pets; no smoking indoors; French understood; Visa/MasterCard. La Midi, a French restaurant nearby, is highly recommended, as is Garibaldi's for Northern Italian cuisine and Anson's for a gourmet experience.

DIRECTIONS: downtown Charleston 3 blocks off King Street.

TWO MEETING STREET INN

Charleston's gem

What a wedding gift! In 1890, George Walton Williams gave his daughter $75,000 to build this magnificent Queen Anne mansion and then packed the honeymoon couple off to Europe for two years to await its completion. Not to be outdone, the family of the groom presented the couple with exquisite Tiffany windows emblazoned with royal purple irises for their fifth anniversary. Tiffany himself accompanied his handiwork to Charleston to oversee its installation.

Years later when the family sold the house, a neighbor who had always admired it, bought it. Many of her family heirlooms remain today, along with other notable historic items acquired by her descendants and present innkeepers, the Spell family.

Throughout the house, intricately carved oak paneling enriches everything. Highlights in the parlor include an unusually tall Renaissance Revival étagère, one of a pair of cut glass and brass gas-lit chandeliers, a bas-relief fireplace, and David Spells' wonderful collection of Canton china. The dining room, with its brilliant stained-glass scallop shell window, Chippendale dining room furniture, and sterling silver is an elegant setting for breakfast in winter.

Eight guest rooms on three floors, with a parlor on each, evoke romantic reveries. The room on the first floor was converted from the men's parlor into the Pink Room, and is awash in pinks, pale lemon, and maroon. The Blue Room on the second level has a wonderful corn-flower blue bas-relief tile fireplace, red velvet wing chairs, and a fishnet canopied tester Charleston rice bed. A door leads to the second-floor verandah.

Outdoors, there are two tiers of wrap-around verandahs and a piazza shaded by live oaks, where breakfast is served. All overlook the Battery and waterfront where the Ashley and Cooper Rivers flow into the Atlantic Ocean.

The glorious homes built by yesterday's prosperous merchants fill the immediate vicinity of the inn and can best be seen on foot or by carriage.

Surely wedding gifts like Two Meeting Street Inn ensure that marriages will last forever.

TWO MEETING STREET INN, 2 Meeting Street, Charleston, SC 29401; (803) 723-7322; the Spell Family, owners. Closed for 3 days at Christmas. 9 guest rooms, with private baths. Rates: $105 to $175 per room, including continental breakfast. Children over 8 welcome; no pets; no smoking; German spoken; no credit cards, personal checks accepted.

DIRECTIONS: follow Meeting Street all the way down to South Battery.

The Blue Room.

ALL PHOTOGRAPHS BY WILLIAM STRUHS

The Elizabeth Grimké Room, named after John Rutledge's wife, is on the second floor along with the John Rutledge Suite and the Ballroom.

JOHN RUTLEDGE HOUSE INN

Elegant living on a grand scale

The grandness of word and deed that manifested itself in early American history sprang from great men of high intellect and unbounded energy. The John Rutledge House is dedicated to these men, room by room, floor by floor, with portraits and memorabilia of each. The grand spaces, high ceilings, and intricately parqueted floors of this great house attest to the grand scale on which these first Americans lived.

The ground floor honors the signers of the Constitution from North Carolina, one of whom was John Rutledge's brother, whose own house sits directly across the street.

The first floor honors military men who stayed at the house or visited there for meetings while plotting the Revolution. No dank cellars for these men (one of whom was George Washington), but, instead, elegantly appointed rooms like the Grand Ballroom, which is now a beautiful reception room where guests gather in the afternoons for wine and sherry and conversation.

The second floor honors John Rutledge himself, and his wife Elizabeth. It includes the library where Rutledge wrote the first drafts of the Constitution. He was a signer of the Declaration of Independence, as were other North Carolinians honored on the top floor.

When first built in 1763, the house was Georgian in style. The intricate iron balconies and railings we see on the front today were added in 1853 during reconstruction work. The house is now luxuriously restored, with eight elegantly furnished rooms and three Grand Suites with pocket doors separating bedroom and sitting room. There are also two carriage houses, each with four sumptuous guest rooms.

THE JOHN RUTLEDGE HOUSE INN, 116 Broad Street, Charleston, SC 29401; (803) 723-7999 or (800) 476-9741; Rick Widman, owner-manager. Open all year. 19 guest rooms, all with private baths, some with Jacuzzis. Rates: $100 to $210 single, $125 to $225 double, $285 Grand Suites, including continental breakfast; full breakfast available; all are delivered to rooms. Children welcome; no pets; smoking rooms available; Visa/MasterCard/American Express.

DIRECTIONS: off King Street; free parking in rear.

The inn's rooftop view of Charleston's harbor.

VENDUE INN

A roof with a view

The Vendue Inn is a triumph of the restoration mania that seizes people when they see an old dilapidated building. In this case, Morton and Evelyn Needle turned an abandoned 120-year-old warehouse in Charleston's French Quarter into an eighteen-room haven for weary travelers who want to wake up in the heart of historic Charleston.

The guest rooms are individually furnished with oriental rugs, canopied beds, and reproduction period furniture. Freshly cut flowers grace the rooms, along with complimentary sherry and liqueur with chocolate mints at bedtime.

Afternoons, there is a wine and cheese party in the courtyard, and the rooftop offers a stunning view of the harbor and relaxation in wicker chairs and lounges.

For the ultimate in luxury, the inn has added additional quarters at Vendue West. All the facilities are sumptuous suites with fireplaces, well-stocked wet bars, marble baths, Jacuzzis, eighteenth-century furnishings, and a full breakfast.

Historic Charleston is a mecca for springtime visitors who want to see the fabulous gardens and historic houses for which Charleston is so famous.

The King Street antiques shops are another magnet that make for a pleasant stroll, and the Public Market fronting on Meeting Street offers many inviting stalls offering a variety of goods, ranging from old automobile advertisements and other printed ephemera to a multitude of craft displays.

VENDUE INN, 19 Vendue Range, Charleston, SC 29401; (800) 845-7900 [U.S.]; (800) 922-7900 [S.C. only]; (803) 577-7970; Morton and Evelyn Needle, owners. Open all year. 33 rooms, including 9 suites, all with private baths, 7 with Jacuzzis and fireplaces. Rates vary from $95 single in low season to $135 double in high season; suites from $160 to $220; includes continental breakfast, afternoon wine and cheese, parking. Suites in Vendue West include full breakfast. Children welcome; no pets; smoking allowed; Visa/MasterCard/American Express/Discover.

DIRECTIONS: off East Bay Street at base of Waterfront Park.

Every room is unique

MAISON DUPRÉ

A fabulous complex of preserved buildings

For those attending the Spoleto Art Festival, as well as those touring Magnolia Plantation or Middleton Place, the Maison DuPré offers lodging in Charleston's most splendid tradition.

Performing artists are frequent guests at this inn, which is adjacent to the Gailliard Auditorium where stars like Pavarotti, the Cannes Chamber Orchestra, and the Tulsa Ballet appear regularly. Moreover, the inn is located in the heart of the Ansonborough historic district, making it ideal for tourists and traditional inngoers. Young couples, attracted by the Honeymoon Suite that features a pine sleigh bed, often marry here.

Maison DuPré is comprised of three historic Charleston "singles houses" and two carriage houses that were saved and restored by the owners, Lucille and Bob Mulholland, along with their son, Mark,

who manages the complex. It is centered around a spacious brick courtyard, planted with palmettos, crape myrtles, camellias, roses and cannas, enclosed by a garden wall.

Fifteen rooms with Charleston rice or pencil post twin beds, Oriental carpets, antique armoires, and floral drapes, vie for attention. Their colors, Williamsburg blue, dusty rose, muted gold, and clotted cream, blend harmoniously with artist-owner Lucille Mulholland's paintings of florals, landscapes, and seascapes.

Bob Mulholland says that he and Lucille ended up buying an inn after they'd laughed over *Fawlty Towers*. Innkeeper John Cleese could use Maison DuPré as a blueprint for impeccable innkeeping and hospitality.

MAISON DUPRÉ, 317 East Bay Street, Charleston, SC 29401; (803) 723-8691; Mark Mulholland, manager. Open all year; 12 guest rooms and 3 suites, all with private baths. Rates: $135 to $200 per room, in season, including continental breakfast and Low Country afternoon tea. Children welcome; no pets; smoking outside only; smattering of French spoken; Visa/MasterCard/American Express.

DIRECTIONS: located in the downtown Ansonborough historic district at the corner of East Bay and George Streets. Across the street from the Gailliard Auditorium.

CHICAGO

Old-World charm

It is hard to believe that this handsomely detailed Victorian house, flying the Latvian flag, is located in downtown Chicago. Its spacious backyard, home to a cherry tree, is aglow with peonies, bachelor's buttons, tiger lilies, and roses, that provide floral bouquets for the house. Strawberries and raspberries are picked in season and appear at the breakfast table in fruit cups, accompanied by delicious muffins and scones.

Furnishings are elegant with special appointments such as hand-painted sinks, Sherle Wagner fixtures, Belgian lace cloths, antique paintings, crimson leather chairs, and white lace bedspreads. Two guest rooms are furnished in an artfully eclectic style while the ever-so-spacious apartment on the third floor is modern in décor. It is painful to think that this lovely house had to be heavily fought over to be saved from the wrecker's ball.

Built in 1884, this house is unusual, because there are not many houses left in downtown Chicago. In 1861, the great Chicago fire left more than three square miles in ruins.

Lincoln Park and Lincoln Park Zoo are both nearby and you can bike ride for miles along the lake. There are always festivals and fairs and the widest choice of interesting restaurants imaginable.

The Latvian vice-president stayed here as do many Europeans. No wonder. The house exudes old world charm and the host is gracious and perfectly charming.

The breakfast room.

LINCOLN PARK. 2 guest rooms and 1 apartment with private baths. Open all year. Rates: $65 single, $75 double, $125 apt., including continental breakfast. Well-behaved children over 6 welcome; no pets; no smoking; Latvian spoken. *Represented by Bed & Breakfast/ Chicago Inc.* P.O. Box 14088, Chicago, IL 60614-0088; (312) 951-0085; Mary Shaw. Visa/MasterCard/American Express.

DIRECTIONS: given on reservation.

What a view!

CITY VIEW INN

A room with a view

With a choice of rooms overlooking spectacular views of Lake Michigan or the city's distinctive skyline, this 40th floor penthouse in Chicago's financial district pushes bed and breakfast beyond the glass ceiling. Formerly a private club, twenty-two luxuriously oversized rooms have been swathed in elegance and appointed with every comfort including king-sized beds, deep marble tubs, and original art whose provenance the staff can provide.

Include in this a state-of-the-art health club—30,000 square feet, that offers not only treadmills, StairMasters, Jacuzzi, whirlpools, racquetball, but beyond that a white marble steam room and white marble pool.

A hearty buffet breakfast with everything from breakfast cereals to omelets or waffles is included, or a continental breakfast that is brought to your room. Room service is available until 11:00 P.M. There is critical acclaim for the 5-star French restaurant in the building and the Grill Room allows smoking.

Underground parking is complimentary.

Built in 1886 in the heyday of elaborately magnificent structures, this skyscraper is one of Chicago's finest. Nearby are the Art Institute, Orchestra Hall, Sears Tower, and City Hall.

CITY VIEW INN. 22 guest rooms with private baths. Open all year. Rates: $115 to $160 per room, including buffet breakfast. No children; no pets; smoking allowed. *Represented by Bed & Breakfast/ Chicago Inc.*, P.O. Box 14088, Chicago, IL 60614-0088; (312) 951-0085; Mary Shaw. Visa/MasterCard/American Express.

DIRECTIONS: given on reservation.

A luxurious suite.

CHENEY HOUSE

Architecture by Frank Lloyd Wright

For Frank Lloyd Wright devotées, this is a dream come true—an opportunity to stay in the Cheney House, a home that he designed between 1903 and 1904. Called the "Good Times" house by the architect himself, some have called it Wright's greatest work of Prairie-style architecture.

The house looks much the same today except for the high walls along three sides. Appearing to rise from the ground as a one-level dwelling, it has two levels and an attic.

Inside the house, ceilings vary in height, creating a variety of moods—spaciousness, height, warmth, and isolation. There are intricate patterns of wood-work, and the main level is windowed entirely in art glass.

All of the furniture currently in the house was designed by Wright, but it is not contemporary to the house. It is furniture Wright designed in the 50's for the Heritage-Henredon furniture company. Most pieces exhibit a square with Wright's initials woodburned into them. The china in the living room was designed for the Imperial Hotel in Japan. The twin beds which occupy one of the guest rooms are possibly the first known platform beds.

A photo of Wright taken during a visit to the house in 1956 hangs in the dining room entrance.

A pool table original to the house.

After the house's completion, the Cheney House continued to attract Wright's attention. Whether he was attracted by the house or by Mrs. Cheney is unknown, but the relationship between the two became so public and scandalous that they left to live together in Europe. On their return, Wright built his personal dream house for Mamah Cheney in Taliesin in Wisconsin, where they lived together until she was murdered several years later by a crazed servant.

CHENEY HOUSE, 520 North East Avenue, Oak Park, IL 60302; (708) 524-2067; Dale L. Smirl, owner. Open all year. Two rooms with shared bath and 1 master suite with sitting room and bath. Rates: $100 rooms, $150 suite, including continental breakfast; 2 night minimum stay. Children welcome; no pets; no smoking; no credit cards. Eight very fine restaurants within walking distance. Frank Lloyd Wright's original studio and home nearby, as is the Unitarian Church's Unity Temple, designed by Wright.

DIRECTIONS: Oak Park is the first suburb west of Chicago off the Eisenhower Expressway. Take Harlem Avenue exit to Chicago avenue. Go east on Chicago to East Ave. and turn left to house.

DALLAS / FORT WORTH

Individually luxurious.

THE STOCKYARDS HOTEL

Bonnie and Clyde slept here

An extravaganza of the Western style greets guests at the Stockyards Hotel. Twelve-foot-high pressed tin ceilings, floors covered in terra cotta tiles and rugs handwoven with original Western geometric designs, leather covered chesterfield sofas, steer skins, carved wood chairs, and bar stools topped with saddles are all blended together by designer Kay Howard with the utmost discrimination.

Equally tasteful are the guest rooms, which feature four themes: Indian, Mountain Man, Victorian, and Western. Cedar, slate, deerskins, cattle skulls, ram's head lamps, wormwood shutters, massive armoires, and beautifully designed bedspreads are combined with quiet dignity.

A special guest room is the Bonnie and Clyde Suite, which once hosted the famous duo. On exhibit is Bonnie Parker's personal pistol.

The thoughtful owners have also provided suites for business meetings and special accommodations for families.

Located in the heart of the Fort Worth Stockyards Historic District, all of the district's attractions are immediately available. One that should be mentioned is Billy Bob's Texas, the world's largest honky-tonk, under a 100,000 square foot roof, where entertainment's big names present country, rock, and big band music.

THE STOCKYARDS HOTEL, P.O. Box 4558, Fort Worth, TX 76106; (800) 423-8417; (817) 625-6427; Mike Davis, manager. Open all year. 52 rooms, including 7 suites, all with private baths. Rates: B&B special $110 double, including cowhand breakfast for 2 and parking; deluxe B&B $140 in Bonnie and Clyde's room includes champagne; Suites $350. Children welcome; no pets; smoking allowed; all major credit cards. Located in the heart of the Stockyards Historic District, with all its restaurant and recreation amenities.

DIRECTIONS: from I-35 west take NE 28th Street exit west for 1½ miles to Main Street. Turn left on Main to Exchange and left again to hotel.

MISS MOLLY'S HOTEL

Good golly, Miss Molly!

Authentic is the only word to describe Miss Molly's, a turn-of-the-century boarding house and latterly a brothel in the second largest stockyards and meat packing town in the country.

Owners Mark and Susan Hancock have recreated that era with the help of the North Fort Worth Historical Society, including the exact furniture and fixtures of the time. Hot baths used to be charged extra, and a big improvement is that today they are included as part of the standard room rates, although the bathrooms, with their claw-foot tubs, are still down the hall.

The rooms have themes that give you an idea of the hotel's former customers: oil men, cattle barons, drovers, cowboys, and gun slingers. Along with the shutters, lace curtains, iron beds with antique quilts, and old oak furniture, you get a feeling for life at the turn-of-the-century in a mid-west cow town.

Nearby, old-time saloons, western shops, galleries, and colorful restaurants provide more than enough amenities, in addition to all the regularly scheduled Fort Worth activities.

Some of the outstanding activities include the indoor rodeo at the Cowtown Coliseum, the Tarantula Steam Train to the Fort Worth Stockyards, where the Old West lives on, the Sid Richardson Collection of Western Art, the Log Cabin Village, the Amon Carter Museum of Western and American art, the Cattleman's Museum of ranch life in the Southwest, the Fort Worth Museum of Science and History, and the Noble Planetarium. There are also the Fort Worth Zoo, the Botanic Garden, and the Arlington Theme Parks with their roller coasters, wax museums and so forth to add spice to your visit to fabulous Fort Worth.

MISS MOLLY'S HOTEL, 109½ West Exchange Avenue, Fort Worth, TX 76106; (817) 626-1522; Susan Hancock, manager. Open all year. Eight rooms, including 1 suite with private bath and sitting room, and 7 rooms with shared baths. Rates: $68 per room, suite $125, all including deluxe continental breakfast. Children 6 and over welcome; no pets; no smoking; Visa/MasterCard/American Express/Diners Club/Discover. Twelve excellent dining places in area, including Risky's Bar BQ, Las Vaqueros, Cattleman's Steak House.

DIRECTIONS: from I-35 west take NE 28th street exit west to North Main Street, which will take you to the Stockyards Historic District.

The Cowboy Room

Miss Josie's Room.

HOTEL ST. GERMAIN

Unsurpassed luxury

In a modern city like Dallas, better known for its concrete high-rises, the Hotel St. Germain is a rare jewel.

Built in 1906 just north of downtown Dallas, the three-story white house is actually a full service luxury hotel. It has only seven suites, but they are the most sumptuous accommodations you could possibly find. As for the rest of the interior, well . . . have you ever seen Versailles?

Elaborate chandeliers hang from the high ceilings of the entrance hall and dining room beyond. The tall windows are draped with rich fabrics copied from nineteenth-century French designs. The woodwork trim has been treated with a rich crackle-back effect, and all the floors are polished wood. Moss-green French antiques and Bordeaux red patterns blend exquisitely with gold accents. Some of the screens and tapestries are over two hundred years old. There is also a formal parlor, library, and an intimate New Orleans-style courtyard.

Left. *The monumental Suite Two.*

The St. Germain is the brainchild of Claire Heymann, a native of Louisiana, who recently saved the house from demolition and restored it to an unsurpassed state of luxury. The décor reflects her French-Creole background, and it is clear that no expense was spared.

In addition to a full-time concierge, valet parking, and turn-down service, the St. Germain also offers gourmet candlelight dinners served on seventy-five-year-old Limoges china by tuxedoed butlers. The butlers reappear in the morning to serve café au lait and homebaked pastries.

The second and third floors house seven suites, each one more lavish than the next. They all have canopied feather beds, elegant French antiques, working fireplaces, large pristine bathrooms (some with pedestal sinks and Jacuzzi tubs), Roger and Gallet soaps, and guest robes. Some of the balconies capture city views.

HOTEL ST. GERMAIN, 2516 Maple Avenue, Dallas, TX 75201; (214) 871-2516; Claire L. Heymann, owner. Open all year. AAA ◆ ◆ ◆ ◆ rating. Seven suites, all with private baths and fireplaces; some rooms with Jacuzzi tubs. Rates: $200 to $600, including continental-plus breakfast. Children not encouraged; no pets; non-smoking rooms available; French and Spanish spoken. Visa/MasterCard/American Express. Dining room on premises open to the public on weekends; open to guests for dinner all week with advance notice. In heart of McKinney Avenue District, with 50 restaurants, 25 art galleries, and 25 antique shops within walking distance.

DIRECTIONS: Located just north of downtown Dallas between McKinney Ave. and Cedar Springs. Directions given upon confirmation.

DENVER

Jim and Diane Peiker in their garden.

CASTLE MARNE

A treasure trove

Built in 1889 and restored a century later, Castle Marne is one of Denver's finest urban inns. The magnificent stone structure was built by famous architect William Lang, who also built the ("Unsinkable") Molly Brown House. Castle Marne offers guests hospitality and comfort amid a wealth of fascinating historical treasures and memorabilia.

Jim and Diane Peiker own the inn, and operate it with their children as a family business. The result is a winning blend of Old-World charm, Victorian elegance, modern convenience, and personal service. Whether guests seek recommendations on local attractions, details about the Castle's history, or a romantic candle-light dinner, the Peikers and their staff are ready, willing, and able to comply.

Each of the nine guest rooms is uniquely decorated

Left above. The opulent drawing room. Below. The breakfast table glistens with silver service.

with authentic period antiques, family heirlooms, and fine-quality reproductions. The sunny and elegant John T. Mason Suite has a brass bed, highboy dresser, cathedral ceiling, jet whirlpool tub, and an amazing, museum-quality butterfly collection.

Complete gourmet breakfasts are served in the original, cherry-paneled, formal dining room, where guests savor homemade breads, muffins, blueberry pancakes, quiche, Belgian waffles, Marne-blend coffee, tea, and a variety of other epicurean delights, all presented on china, silver, and crystal. Treats are served in the late afternoon on the airy veranda or in the parlor.

People walking by are mysteriously drawn to the door of this magnificent and compelling building.

CASTLE MARNE, 1572 Race Street, Denver, CO 80206; (303) 331-0621, (800) 92-MARNE; FAX (303) 331-0623; Jim & Diane Peiker, owners; Melissa Feher-Peiker, innkeeper. Open all year. Seven rooms and two suites, with private baths, ceiling fans, and whirlpool tubs in suites. Rates: $70 to $165 single, $85 to $165 double with full gourmet breakfast; gift shop. Children over 10 welcome; no pets; no smoking; Visa/MasterCard/American Express/Diner's Club/Discover; Hungarian spoken. Guest office facilities with computer, typewriter, etc. Excellent dining within walking distance.

DIRECTIONS: from the intersection of US-40 (Colfax Ave.) and York St., go west 4 blocks to Race St., then one block north.

The inn is composed of two houses.

QUEEN ANNE INN

A romantic getaway

Serenely located on the edge of busy downtown Denver, the Queen Anne has the romantic look and feel of a nineteenth-century country inn. It occupies two side-by-side historic homes which exemplify the Queen Anne style of Victorian architecture and are set among other beautifully restored homes comprising the Clements Historic District.

Choosing to stay at the Queen Anne Inn is the easy part. Deciding which of its many beautifully appointed rooms or suites you want to call "home" during your sojourn is much more difficult. One Victorian houses ten double rooms, each wonderfully decorated and furnished with period antiques.

The Aspen Room is the most photographed. It features a unique, hand-painted-in-the-round mural of an aspen grove extending from the floor all the way up to the turret peak. Other rooms to choose from have such colorful names as Fountain, Tower, Skyline, Columbine, Rooftop, Park, Garden, Tabor, and Oak—suggestive of each room's unique view and décor. All rooms have private baths, telephones,

writing desks, piped-in chamber music (Vivaldi, Mozart, Segovia, etc.), and fresh flowers.

Next door there are four contemporary "Gallery Suites," each dedicated to one of the innkeeper's favorite artists—Norman Rockwell, Frederick Remington, Alexander Calder, and John James Audubon. These gloriously decorated, luxury suites offer guests distinctly individual and incomparable urban-inn experiences.

A buffet-style breakfast is served for two hours each morning and includes fresh fruit, juice, granola, muffins, warm croissants, pancakes, waffles, and the innkeeper's hot entrée—quiche (two varieties daily).

Longtime innkeeper Tom King purchased the inn in 1992 and created a masterpiece that has been named one of Colorado's seven most romantic getaway destinations.

QUEEN ANNE INN, 2147 Tremont Place, Denver, CO 80205; (303) 296-6666, (800) 432-4667 (outside of Colorado only); FAX (303) 296-2151; Tom King, innkeeper. Open all year. Ten double rooms and four suites, with private baths with deep soaker tubs or jet tubs. Rates: $75 to $145, including full breakfast, free off-street parking, and early-evening refreshments. Children over 12 welcome; no pets; no smoking; Visa/MasterCard/American Express/Discover; Spanish, French spoken. Fine dining nearby. Central to all downtown locations.

DIRECTIONS: from east on US-40 (Colfax Ave.) and west on US-6, turn north onto Logan St. to 20th Ave. (where Logan ends at the park), turn left ½ block to Tremont Pl. and turn right ½ block to Inn.

HAUS BERLIN

Exemplary hosts

The three words that best capture the essence of Haus Berlin are *bright, airy,* and *friendly.*

Dennis and Christiana Brown restored and renovated this Victorian townhouse to produce one of the most inviting and comfortable bed and breakfasts in Denver. Situated in the northwest part of Denver's Swallow Hill Historic District, Haus Berlin is a small and intimate inn, run by a couple who cut their teeth on hosting guests in the Virgin Islands.

Dennis did the refinishing, and Christiana took charge of the decorating to convert the building from a dark, typically Victorian décor to the bright and airy ambiance it now possesses—that lifts the spirits and makes visitors feel right at home. A stay at Haus Berlin is like a visit with old friends. The hosts are the quintessential innkeepers. Their guests' comfort is their first, last, and only concern. Even "Puddy Cat," the resident feline, is attentive to the inn's guests.

Continental breakfasts have "that special touch." Guests love the fresh-baked breads, waffles with caramel sauce, herbal tea, or melon balls with honey glaze and spiced with ginger.

That third-floor suite is inviting enough to make you want to disappear up there for a week, or maybe two.

All linens are luxurious, 100-percent cotton, and ironed by hand, and beds all have cozy, warm, down-filled comforters.

Each second-floor room is beautifully appointed and furnished, complete with fresh-cut flowers. The third-floor suite can comfortably accommodate up to three adults. It is the essence of luxury, with elegant bedding and décor, a double shower, and even a bidet.

HAUS BERLIN, 1651 Emerson Street, Denver, CO 80218; Voice & FAX: (303) 837-9527; Dennis & Christiana Brown, hosts. Open all year. Four rooms with queen or king-sized beds and private baths. Rates: $85 to $110, including continental breakfast. No children; no pets; no smoking; Visa/MasterCard/American Express; German spoken. Wide selection of fine dining nearby. Denver City Park, Museum of Natural History, Denver City Zoo, State Capitol building, Molly Brown House, the Denver Mint, and downtown Denver in area.

DIRECTIONS: from the intersection of US-40 (Colfax Ave.) and Colorado Blvd., take Colfax west to Emerson St., turn right on Emerson 1½ blocks to Haus Berlin on left.

MERRITT HOUSE

A B&B / restaurant

When Mary and Tom Touris purchased the Merritt House in 1986, they began a painstaking restoration to preserve the house's historical character, while bringing it up to city codes. In recognition of that remarkable accomplishment, they received the Colorado Preservation Society's Award for Excellence.

A solid-oak staircase leads up to the guest rooms on the second and third floors. Each room is unique, with either a four-poster, brass, or sleigh bed, wing-back chairs, oriental carpet, and armoire.

The Merritt House has its own intimate restaurant which serves breakfast, brunch, and lunch. Delicious morning meals offer bacon, ham, country sausage, and a variety of egg dishes (including, of course, the ever-popular *Denver omelet*), as well as strawberry or blueberry pancakes, hot or cold cereals, and French toast.

MERRITT HOUSE, 941 E. 17th Avenue, Denver, CO 80218; (303) 861-5230; Tom & Mary Touris, owners. Open all year. Ten rooms with queen-sized beds, 9 with private baths, some with Jacuzzis, one with bath across hall. Rates: $80 to $95 single; $90 to $125 double; includes full breakfast. Children over 12; no pets; no smoking in public areas; Visa/MasterCard/American Express; American sign language.

DIRECTIONS: from the intersection of US-40 (Colfax Ave.) and Colorado Blvd., take Colfax west to Emerson St., turn right on Emerson and go 2 blocks to 17th Ave., turn right on 17th, and go 1 block to the Merritt House.

A guest room.

A guest suite.

MANY MANSIONS

Pure comfort

No antiques, no bric-a-brac, just pure contemporary comfort. That's what Many Mansions' 36 fully furnished roomy, well-appointed suites provide for guests, only a few minutes from downtown Denver.

Every suite has a well-equipped kitchen with all the major appliances and utensils you need to prepare anything from a boiled egg to a gourmet feast. The housekeeping staff cleans each suite daily, including your dishes.

American breakfasts are provided by a caterer each weekday morning in the Club Room on the eighth floor, just a short elevator ride away. Breakfasts may include eggs, French toast, pancakes, English muffins, bagels, toast, coffee, tea, etc. Continental breakfasts are provided on weekends. When the weather permits, meals may be enjoyed on the outdoor patio.

Treats are available in the lobby throughout the day: mid-afternoon tea and biscuits, sherry at 5:00 P.M., and freshly-baked cookies at 7:30 P.M.

MANY MANSIONS, 1313 Steele Street, Denver, CO 80206-2549; (303) 355-1313; (800) 225-7829; Jim Kraft, general manager. Open all year. 36 one and two-bedroom suites with private baths. Rates: $90 to $145; senior discounts. Includes cable TV, and full breakfast. Children under 12 free; no pets; limited smoking; saunas; all major credit cards. Free weekday transportation provided (subject to advance scheduling) within limited areas for shopping, recreation, airport, and downtown.

DIRECTIONS: from south on I-25 take Colorado Blvd. exit for 3 miles north to 13th, then 8 blocks west; from north on I-25 take Colfax exit for 3½ miles east to Steele, then 1 block south.

KANSAS CITY

The striking entrance hall.

A guest room.

WYNBRICK INN B&B

Harry Truman played poker here

Located about ten miles outside Kansas City, Wynbrick is uniquely set up as both a B&B and clubhouse for the newly-built homes in the neighborhood. Guests and residents alike have use of the inn's club room, exercise room, and pool. The expansive lawn and courtyard in back are also the site of many wedding celebrations.

Built in 1928 by Howard Hall, this brick mansion was once a secluded estate. It is said that Harry Truman used to come over to play poker in the basement when he was a judge. Before it was turned into a B&B in 1990, the whole mansion was completely restored into its now-pristine state. Hand-milled archways, a graceful staircase, original built-ins, and luxurious bathrooms are found throughout. Many of the arched windows feature folding shutters and lovely window treatments.

Guest rooms, most named after famous Clay County figures, manage to display individual personalities (each was decorated by a different designer) without seeming cluttered. The Jesse James Room, for example, has a Western feel with its wood floors, leather saddle, and "Wanted" handbill. Another room features Civil War memorabilia, an iron bed, and old chests. (The town of Liberty was once a Civil War stronghold. Until well into the twentieth century, the Confederate flag flew beneath the American Flag at the local courthouse.)

In the winter, fireplaces warm the living room and dining room, where a continental breakfast is served each morning.

WYNBRICK INN BED & BREAKFAST, 1701 WynBrick Drive, Liberty, MO 64068; (816) 781-4900; Tamara Taylor, manager. Open all year. Four rooms and one suite, all with private baths. Rates: $55 to $85, including continental-plus breakfast and evening refreshments. Club room and exercise room. Children welcome; no pets; smoking allowed on first floor only; Visa/MasterCard/American Express. Wedding and reception facilities available. Sports stadium, shopping, and Worlds of Fun Amusement Park nearby.

DIRECTIONS: from I-35, take exit 16 east to Liberty; turn right at Conistor and continue to first 4-way stop. Turn left on Liberty Dr. for one block to entrance.

SOUTHMORELAND

A world class bed and breakfast

Southmoreland on the Plaza is one of those rare finds—a first-rate inn that has all the personal touches of a B&B and the sophisticated amenities of a hotel. The innkeepers—Susan Moehl, Penni Johnson and their staff—are friendly and fun yet thoroughly professional. In short, Southmoreland has something for everyone, from first-time inn-goers to seasoned travelers, from single business people to romantic couples.

Built in 1913, this Colonial Revival mansion was transformed by Susan and Penni into a polished, New-England-style inn. At the same time they added many cutting-edge conveniences and complete business facilities. In the library-like den, a television, VCR and choice of one hundred movies (all with happy endings) are hidden discreetly behind an armoire. The sunny solarium, with its white wicker and crisp blue accents, is particularly inviting.

Each guest room is named after a Kansas City notable and has been meticulously decorated in the era and personality of the namesake. For example,

Left. Two of the guest rooms.

the Leroy "Satchel" Paige Room, rustically furnished with baseball memorabilia on the walls, comes complete with tickets to the Royals home games.

Some rooms feature double Jacuzzis, or fireplaces, or private decks ranging from large to "martini"-sized. Other luxuries include down comforters and pillows, spotless, white-tiled bathrooms, special soaps, telephones with round-the-clock reception, and complimentary aperitifs. While enjoying wine and hors d'oeuvres, your bed is turned down. In the morning, the newspaper is left quietly outside your door.

Guests are offered three breakfast choices—light, American-style, or gourmet. The gourmet meal is pretty irresistible: A typical menu—apricot-banana frappés, orange-pecan wheat germ bread, and French toast stuffed with sugar-cured ham and Lorraine-Swiss.

SOUTHMORELAND ON THE PLAZA, 116 E. 46th Street, Kansas City, MO 64112; (816) 531-7979; FAX (816) 531-2407; Susan Moehl and Penni Johnson, owners. Open all year. Twelve rooms (one designed for the physically handicapped), all with private baths. Rates: $90 to $135, including evening hors d'oeuvres and full breakfast. Children over 12 welcome; no pets; limited smoking; Visa/MasterCard/American Express. Membership privileges at historic Rockhill Tennis Club included. Full business facilities. Grand Street, Cape Allegro, Vecos, and Venue recommended for dining. Nelson-Atkins Museum of Art, Art Institute, Country Club Plaza, Royals Baseball, and Chiefs Football nearby.

DIRECTIONS: from I-70, I-35, and I-29 in downtown Kansas City, exit at Main St., proceed south several miles to east 46th St. and turn left. Inn is 1½ blocks on left.

The entry hall.

DOANLEIGH WALLAGH INN

Super breakfasts

The most frequent thing guests say about Doanleigh Wallagh is that it is both elegant and comfortable at the same time—a hard balance for most B&B's to manage.

The "comfortable" part of staying here is due in large part to hosts Carolyn and Ed Litchfield. They are naturals at innkeeping—friendly and welcoming, with a knack for making their guests feel immediately at ease.

The elegance of this 1907 Georgian mansion—the first B&B in Kansas City—comes from the spacious rooms, chandeliers, and stately Georgian antiques found throughout. In the formal living room, for instance, red leather wingback chairs sit before a fireplace that blazes in the winter. A grand piano, which guests are encouraged to play, awaits in the corner. And on the wall is a distinguished portrait of Ed's great, great, great grandmother Sarah Doanleigh, who once lived on the Welsh estate called Wallagh.

But Ed and Carolyn have made even their most

Left, above. A large guest room with a fireplace.
Below. Another large guest room.

elegant guest room—the Hyde Park Room, with its splendid antique desk, four-poster bed, wood-burning fireplace, and large armoire—a comfortable place for guests. Inside the armoire, a television is surrounded by stuffed teddy bears. ("Some guests let them out!" says Carolyn, in mock indignity.) Homemade cookies are set out temptingly on the table.

The Litchfields cook a super breakfast, including such scrumptious delights as Apples in a Comforter (a German pancake), stuffed French toast, Russian pancakes, and eggs Benedict. They allow their guests to select the breakfast time and the choice between a full or light meal.

Doanleigh Wallagh is situated in the Hyde Park district—a three-block parkway flanked by large, turn-of-the-century homes. It is conveniently close to downtown Kansas City, the art museums, and Country Club Plaza.

DOANLEIGH WALLAGH INN, 217 E. 37th Street, Kansas City, MO 64111; (816) 753-2667; FAX (816) 753-2408; Carolyn and Edward Litchfield, owners-innkeepers. Open all year. Five rooms, all with private baths. Rates: $80 to $110, including full breakfast and complimentary snack bar. Reception and meeting facilities available. Children welcome; no pets; smoking allowed only on first floor; Visa/MasterCard/American Express. Classic Cup and Cafe Nile recommended for dining. The innkeepers highly recommend seeing the Steamboat Arabia Museum in addition to the usual Kansas City sights.

DIRECTIONS: Three blocks east of Main St. on the corner of 37th St. and Gillham Rd.

LOS ANGELES

The Americana Attic Suite on the third floor.

SALISBURY HOUSE B&B

Classic Craftsman

This 1909 California Craftsman house, the first bed and breakfast in Los Angeles, is centrally located in the historic West Adams district near downtown—a once-affluent neighborhood which fell into decline after the Santa Monica Freeway cut through it. Although visitors may be put off by the surrounding area, all is forgotten when you turn onto spacious 20th Street and enter the oasis of the Salisbury House.

Used as a location for several movie productions, the Salisbury House is a refreshing sight. Classic Craftsman-style wood beams outline the immaculately restored home, while jacarandas, roses, and bougainvillea bloom at the entry. The large living room and dining room feature an abundance of wood paneling, wood-beamed ceilings, original leaded glass and whimsical light fixtures.

The dining room table is nicely set for breakfast

Left. The front entrance, blooming with jacarandas, roses, and bougainvillea.

with a lace tablecloth, white linens, and pink Depression glass. Breakfast specialties include strawberry waffles, spicy Mexican casseroles with cornbread, and country casseroles with potatoes and fresh herbs from the herb garden in back.

The second-floor guest rooms are fresh and floral, with old-fashioned furnishings and lots of nice decorative touches.

SALISBURY HOUSE BED & BREAKFAST, 2273 W. 20th Street, Los Angeles, CA 90018; (213) 737-7817; (800) 373-1778; Sue and Jay German, innkeepers. Open all year. Five rooms and suites, two with shared bath. Rates: $70 to $95, single; $75 to $100, double, including full breakfast. Children accepted; no pets; no smoking; some Spanish and French spoken; Visa/MasterCard/American Express/Discover. Inn is 10 to 20 minutes from every major sight in Los Angeles. A restaurant guide, written by the innkeeper, is available.

DIRECTIONS: one block north of I-10 between Western and Arlington Streets.

Innkeeper Sue German.

LA MAIDA HOUSE

North Hollywood Mediterranean villa

Italian artisans, brought here in the 1920s, adorned this seven-thousand-square-foot Sicilian mansion with ironwork, woodwork, marble, and fountains. Built on a grand scale, it is a villa not unlike those found on the Mediterranean.

The splendor of magnolia trees, blooming orchids, and three hundred varieties of roses can be viewed from the stained-glass-covered solarium, while the grace of a former era is reflected in the expansive living room and a dining room that seats thirty-four. There are several casual niches for relaxing, among them a multi-tiered couch in the game room and an upstairs porch for intimate dining.

The rooms, filled with fresh exotic flowers from La Maida's gardens, are airy and elegant. An especially glorious one, in the main house, is the Cipresso Suite, with a white-canopied four-poster bed, wicker chaise, mirrored dressing room, and large blue-tiled bathroom. Downstairs the sun pours through white lace curtains, creating beautiful shadows at arched windows. Adding to the warmth are the stained-glass windows designed and made by Megan Timothy, La Maida's hostess.

The windows only hint at Megan's artistry, for in addition to working with clay, stone, and fabric, she is a highly skilled cook. A beautifully presented continental breakfast is an introduction to epicurean dinners that Megan can arrange and prepare for guests. She also makes her own jams and marmalades from the grapevines and fruit trees that thrive on the grounds.

LA MAIDA HOUSE & BUNGALOWS, 11159 La Maida Street, North Hollywood, CA 91601; (818) 769-3857; FAX (818) 753-9363. Megan Timothy, hostess. Four rooms in main house; seven in bungalows, all with private entrances, and several with Jacuzzi tubs and private gardens. Rates: $85 to $210, including generous continental breakfast. Business and social affairs arranged. No pets; no smoking; no credit cards. Close to most major movie studios.

DIRECTIONS: Please call ahead.

WILL FALLER

The Fontana Room, which has extra-long beds.

The Pier Suite.

VENICE BEACH HOUSE

Romantic lodgings near the beach

This restored house by the sea is a survivor of the splendid era of expansive two-story shingled beach houses and a more carefree way of life. Whether it is the breeze off the ocean, just steps away, or the easy hospitality of innkeeper Betty Lou Weiner, one feels privileged to have discovered the Venice Beach House.

Photographs of early Venice hang in the hallways, reminding guests of the days when this strip of Los Angeles marshland was turned into a simulation of Venice, Italy, complete with canals, bathhouses and boardwalks. Guest rooms are named after the eccentric characters who were instrumental in the resort's rise and subsequent decline.

The mood shifts from the contemporary elegance of the Pier Suite, a cool gray accented with rose, to Cora's Corner, a romantic pink and white wicker room. The room named after town father Abbott Kinney is covered in Scottish plaid wool, hunter green carpet, and dark wainscoting.

An additional pleasure is bathing side by side in a large, lush bathroom in claw-foot tubs, or enjoying the double Jacuzzi in James Peasgood's Room.

Breakfast on the veranda or in the sunny bay-window parlor usually includes cheeses, tomatoes, and meats as well as fruit, granola and a variety of breads.

You'll feel quite comfortable here. The inn is an informal, lovely place in which to relax near the sea, and is quietly situated on a pedestrian-only walkway.

VENICE BEACH HOUSE, No. 15 Thirtieth Avenue, Venice, CA 90291; (310) 823-1966. Betty Lou Weiner, innkeeper. Open all year. Nine rooms, five with private bath. Rates: $80 to $150, including expanded continental breakfast and afternoon refreshments. Children welcome; smoking permitted in porch areas; Visa/MasterCard/American Express. Kifuni and 12 Washington recommended for dining.

DIRECTIONS: from I-405, exit at Washington Street and head towards the ocean. Turn right at Speedway (the last street before the ocean) and the house is on the right corner. Parking in the rear. Ten minutes from LAX.

THE INN AT 657

Five elegant suites

The Inn at 657, the closest bed and breakfast to downtown Los Angeles, was built in the 1930's as an apartment house. Innkeeper Patsy Humiston Carter, a retired trial lawyer, restored the building in 1991 and created five elegant suites complete with goosedown comforters, ironed sheets, bouquets of fresh roses and gladiolus, and refrigerators stocked with homemade goodies.

The suites vary in size and mood. The Oriental Blue Suite, for example, is attractively light, boasting a large living room in teals and corals, with silk furnishings and a Turkish rug. A ceremonial kimono hangs on the wall. The fully equipped kitchen is fresh and spotless.

Down a flowery walkway, in an apartment to the rear, is the dining room, where the table is laid with sterling silver and cut crystal for breakfast. Patsy's love of cooking is one of the reasons she turned to innkeeping. She buys her fruit directly from the downtown produce market and whips up such delights as Italian frittatas with ham, strawberry yogurt, and homemade bread pudding.

The Inn is situated in a neighborhood full of social contrast. Across the street is the elegant campus of Mount St. Mary's College, but also nearby are some pretty gritty areas. It's a fact of life in L.A. that you can't have one extreme without the other, and the Inn provides a safe harbor between the two.

THE INN AT 657, 657 West Twenty-Third Street, Los Angeles, CA 90007; (213) 741-2200; (800) 347-7512. Patsy Humiston Carter, proprietor. Open all year. Rates: $95, double occupancy, including full breakfast. Jacuzzi on the premises. No pets; no smoking; Spanish spoken; no credit cards. Close to USC, Los Angeles Convention Center, financial district, Shrine Auditorium, Civic Center, Music Center. Engine Company No. 28, El Jarrito, and Taylor's Steak House recommended for dining.

DIRECTIONS: from I-110 south, exit at Adams and turn right on 23rd Street. The Inn is one block west of Figueroa.

LORD MAYOR'S INN B&B

Sensitively restored

This pristine blue and white Edwardian house, once the home of the first mayor of Long Beach, was meticulously renovated by Laura and Reuben Brasser.

Throughout the warm wood interior is a mix of family heirlooms and antiques, including fine armoires, rockers and distinctive beds. In Margarita's Room are two eighteenth-century Austrian beds, while the Hawaiian Room features an elaborately carved Hawaiian wedding bed complete with pineapple and hula girl motifs. The many rag rugs over the wood floors were crafted by Laura, as were the window coverings and dried flower arrangements.

The hearty breakfasts range from scrambled eggs and popovers to buttermilk pancakes. Laura makes her coffee cakes, jams and lemon curd from scratch.

All the highlights of downtown Long Beach—the Queen Mary, convention center, World Trade Center and Terrace Theatre—are only minutes away from this historic landmark.

LORD MAYOR'S INN BED & BREAKFAST, 435 Cedar Avenue, Long Beach, CA 90802; (310) 436-0324. Laura and Reuben Brasser, innkeepers. Open all year. Five rooms, all with private baths. Rates: $85 to $95, including a full breakfast and evening refreshments. One-night mystery packages available. Children accepted; no pets; smoking allowed on deck only; Freisian, Dutch and Danish spoken; Visa/MasterCard/American Express. Many good seafood restaurants nearby.

DIRECTIONS: from I-710 south, exit at 6th St. After three blocks, turn right on Cedar Ave. Inn is on the right.

MICHAEL LeROY PHOTOGRAPH

CHANNEL ROAD INN

No expense was spared on the décor

When you step into the serene, lightly-scented living room, it is hard to believe that hectic Los Angeles is just around the corner and that the inn is set one block from the ocean. The innkeepers have an effective antidote for unwinding from city affairs—grab some milk and cookies, then head straight to the beach on one of their bicycles.

The 1910 building, a rare West Coast example of shingle-clad Colonial Revival architecture, was originally built in another neighborhood of Santa Monica for Thomas McCall, a Scottish oil and cattle baron. After being moved to its present location, the house stood abandoned and defaced with graffiti for twelve years until it was lovingly restored by builder Susan Zolla and friends in 1988. From the goose-down pillows and thousand-dollar mattresses to the appliquéd lace bed coverings, no expense has been spared on décor.

Elegant country is the theme throughout this inn.

The exquisite living room features pastel silk furnishings atop a lavender Chinese rug, vases of fresh roses, a Batchelder-tiled fireplace, and a piano covered with framed photos of the McCall family.

The fourteen guest rooms, many with hardwood floors, were inspired by a variety of interior designers. Room Eleven appeals to romantics, with its gauze-canopied antique pine bed. Creamy-colored Room Twelve is tucked away in a quiet corner with an ocean view. Room Seven, in sophisticated gray and black, is a favorite with businessmen. Honeymooners love the fireplace suite and canopy bed in Room Six.

Guests are pampered with terry robes, spacious private bathrooms, and bubble bath; and wine and cheese are served afternoons in a sunny library. An outdoor spa rests against the flowery hillside. Breakfast includes such specialties as chocolate chip coffee cake, homemade müesli, or bread pudding with boysenberries.

CHANNEL ROAD INN, 219 West Channel Road, Santa Monica, CA 90402; (310) 459-1920; FAX (310) 454-9920. Susan Zolla, owner; Kathy Jensen, manager. Open all year. Fourteen rooms with private baths. Rates: $85 to $200, including full breakfast and afternoon refreshments. Children welcome; no pets; smoking outside only; Spanish and French spoken; Visa/MasterCard; handicapped accessible. Half-dozen good to excellent casual restaurants in area.

DIRECTIONS: I-10 west to Pacific Coast Highway (Rte. 1). Drive north for 2 miles to West Channel Road and turn right.

MIAMI

Left. The classic Art Deco exterior and exhuberant Art Deco lobby.

The breakfast room, or you can eat outside on the terrace.

COLONY HOTEL

State-of-the-Art Deco

This is Bed and Breakfast à la Art Deco. In the heart of Miami's Art Deco district the Colony Hotel, newly renovated, embodies the architecture that defined the 1920s. Once featured as Art Moderne in Europe, it was borrowed by Miami's architects, who added a dollop or two of their own.

The design of the buildings, strongly influenced by the great luxury liners of their day, often have the same curvilinear lines, undulating fronts, port holes, steamship-like decks and railings. They are defined by neon lighting that came of age in the twenties.

True to the Art Deco esprit in Miami, the Colony Hotel melds Art Deco and tropical lushness as evidenced in the palm tree and zebra-skinned jewel of a lobby, the 36 pastel hued guest rooms, and the 1930's art bedecked Colony Bistro Restaurant where a continental breakfast is served. This restaurant features such luscious dinner dishes as pompano with red curry coconut sauce and snapper with truffle tomato nage served with sautéed garlic potatoes and avocado butter.

There are six oceanfront rooms available and prices vary according to season. At night the neon-bathed sidewalk café encourages people-watching of the beautiful indigenous and foreign types that flock to Miami Beach.

COLONY HOTEL, 736 Ocean Drive, Miami Beach, FL 33139; (800) 226-5669, (305) 673-0088, FAX (305) 532-0762; Julie Davies, manager. Open all year. 36 rooms with private baths (some tubs, some showers), 6 rooms are oceanfront. Rates: *June 1 to Oct. 14,* (per room) $89, ocean front double $125, ocean front queen $200; Oct. 15 to May 31, (per room) $119, ocean front double $125, ocean front queen $200; continental breakfast included. Children welcome (no cribs available); no pets; smoking allowed; Spanish, French spoken; Visa/MasterCard/American Express/Diners Club. Facing the famous Miami Beach (beach towels available).

DIRECTIONS: on beach in the famous Art Deco section. Call for detailed directions.

An Aldin 36-foot trawler yacht.

The cottage overlooks a swimming pool.

BISCAYNE BAY

Sweet dreams and harbor lights

For those who feel the primeval call of the sea more than others, Miami offers a bed and breakfast aboard an Aldin 36-foot luxury trawler yacht, with an interior completely finished in teakwood.

Oftentimes chartered for trips during the day, it is available evenings and nights for a party of two or a family of four. There is an aft stateroom with shower that sleeps two, a forward V-shaped double berth with shower, and, amidship, a settee that makes into a double bed. It is roomy and compact at the same time.

There is a dinette amidship where a continental breakfast of croissants, fruit, and coffee is served. For a more substantial repast, and for dinner, there is a Mariott hotel at the marina, while the Omni Mall is next door.

The marina is on Biscayne Bay, just across the causeway and only five minutes from downtown Miami. When not on charter, the personable captain offers a one-hour cruise of Biscayne Bay, where you can have a good look at all the fabulous mansions built on various islands and along the bay.

BISCAYNE BAY. For 1 party of 2 people or family of 4. Available all year. Children welcome (swimmers); no pets; smoking allowed. Rates: $95 double, $10 per extra person. Package including cruise of Biscayne Bay Millionaire's Row $175. *Represented by Bed & Breakfast Co.*, P.O. Box 262, South Miami, FL 33243; (305) 661-3270 phone and FAX; Visa/MasterCard/American Express.
   DIRECTIONS: on reservation.

COCONUT GROVE

Cottage for three

This cottage overlooks a picture postcard pool. Elegantly furnished and appointed with antiques, it is complete with raised hearth and fireplace, and stocked with VCR, microwave, and patio barbecue to grill your own catch of the day. It is located on the secured grounds of a Coconut Grove showplace—a 1916 fifteen-room English Tudor style house.

A welcoming champagne toast greets the well looked after guest amidst royal palms and brilliant bougainvillea. There is a fish pond on the property and a visiting peacock. The hosts are linguists, fluent in Spanish, French, and German.

All of this comfort and beauty is a mere ten minute walk from the heart of Coconut Grove, the home of the fabled Coconut Grove Playhouse, and an abundance of restaurants and cafés with names like Tu Tu Tango, Bernice's Soul Food, and Le Camembert. Famous for its street festivals, popular ones include The Taste of the Grove, and the King Mango Strut, a spoof of the King Orange Jamboree.

COCONUT GROVE. One cottage that sleeps 3, with private bath. Open all year. Rates: $125 for 2, $135 for 3, including deluxe continental breakfast featuring corn bread, lemon and raspberry curd, fresh fruit basket. Children welcome, pets welcome; smoking outdoors only. *Represented by Bed & Breakfast Co.*, P.O. Box 262, South Miami, FL 33243; (305) 661-3270 phone and FAX; Visa/MasterCard/American Express.   DIRECTIONS: on reservation.

A five-acre ranch B&B where horses are also welcome.

HORSE COUNTRY

Bed and breakfast like no other

A walled cherry hedge sets off this five-acre ranch, landscaped with banyans and tropical gardens, where twenty-two horses are boarded and trained. Guests are invited to observe all, while nearby, horses can be rented for riding.

The sprawling ranch house itself is like no other, with its Italian white tile floors, oriental rugs, grand paintings, and unusual antiques. Four elegantly modern guest rooms, and two spacious apartments all have marble bathrooms, whirlpools, and inviting decks. A telescope for skywatching, a pool, good country air, and peaceful quietude make it a welcome retreat for scurrying travelers. It is twenty-five minutes from downtown Miami, twenty minutes from Coconut Grove, and forty-five minutes from the Everglades.

Freshly baked bread, pancakes, waffles, and fresh fruit are typical breakfast dishes. Guests are encouraged to use the ranch's state-of-the-art kitchen to cook up their favorite fare.

For those who cannot abide traveling without their kitty kat, there is a 5-star cat hotel nearby offering classical music. Felines look out on tropical gardens, bird baths, frogs, and lizards through floor-to-ceiling windows.

This bed and breakfast is not what you would expect to find on the outskirts of trendy, hotel-studded Miami Beach. Don't tell too many people about it.

HORSE COUNTRY. Four guest rooms and 2 apartments with private baths and whirlpools. Open all year. Rates: $35 to $65 per room, $50 to $85 for apartments. Continental breakfast, including homemade breads, served in dining room or outside deck. Children 12 and over welcome; cats can be boarded nearby; smoking outdoors only. *Represented by Bed & Breakfast Co.*, P.O. Box 262, South Miami, FL 33243; (305) 661-3270 phone and FAX; Visa/MasterCard/American Express.

DIRECTIONS: on reservation.

Left and above, decorative plaster and tile work mark this period masterpiece.

HOTEL PLACE ST. MICHEL

A Moorish fantasy

Coral Gables, a stone's throw from Miami, is a wonderful small city with lovely shops and flowers everywhere. Well shaded by stately old trees, great live oaks form a leafy arch over Coral Way. Houses with red tile roofs and arched windows and doors exude a Mediterranean flavor. The wealthy build their homes beside golf courses and along canals. Fine five-star restaurants of every ethnic persuasion draw diners, and tennis in Salvadore park and swimming in the 1920s Venetian Pool is a treat.

Originally named the Hotel Seville, Place St. Michel is set on a quiet side street in the heart of Coral Gables. Restored and revived by Stuart Bornstein, the ivy covered building, Moorish in feeling and design, has a gleaming wood interior, vaulted ceilings, and hand-set Spanish tiles. Decorated with English antiques, Oriental rugs, and paddle fans, its rich and dark interior recalls times spent in English country inns.

None of the thirty rooms is alike, but all of their furnishings, paintings, and antiques are carefully chosen. All have armoires and decorative stenciling. There are fresh flowers upon your arrival and a complimentary breakfast when you awake. Room service is available for snacks or more serious dining.

The Restaurant St. Michel is superb, and people from all over the area dine here. There is a street-level piano bar, a rooftop garden, and some fine shops—all adding to the charming ambience of this small hotel.

HOTEL PLACE ST. MICHEL, 162 Alcazar Avenue. Coral Gables, FL 33134; (305) 444-1666; Stuart Bornstein, owner. Open all year; 27 guest rooms, with private baths, telephones and air conditioning. Rates: $99 single, $115 double, $150 suites, including continental breakfast. Children under 12 free, no pets; smoking allowed; Spanish, French, German spoken: Visa/MasterCard/American Express. Minutes from Coconut Grove, theaters, tennis, golf, beaches.

DIRECTIONS: corner of Ponce de Leon and Alcazar in Coral Gables.

MINNEAPOLIS/ST. PAUL

Innkeeper Donna Gustafson.

The Scandinavian Room.

CHATSWORTH B&B

St. Paul's first bed and breakfast

After raising eight children and hosting exchange students from all over the world, Donna and Earl Gustafson missed having lots of people around. In 1986 they converted their handsome Colonial Revival style home into St. Paul's first B&B.

Donna's love of travel is reflected in the various international themes of the well-tended guest rooms. In the Scandinavian Room are cheerful folk-art furnishings that belonged to Donna's Norwegian parents. The African-Asian Room, which has its own deck, is decorated in rattan and grasscloth wallpaper. The mauve-and-blue Victorian Room is a picture of pretty Americana, with flowered wallpaper and a wedding ring quilt on the carved bed.

Guests especially love the luxurious baths at Chatsworth. In the Four-Poster Room, for example, the marble bathroom features a huge double whirlpool. The bath shared by the Oriental and Scandinavian Rooms contains a Japanese soaking tub. Terry robes or kimonos, ample towels, and nice soaps are provided in each room.

A healthful breakfast of yogurt, granola, fresh fruit and muffins is served in a dining room of

Left, below. The dining room has a warm glow from the fine wood paneling.

richly paneled birch. Donna, a nurse-practitioner, is naturally concerned with health and nutrition. She has even converted her basement level into a center for yoga and meditation classes, available to both guests and the local community.

Situated on a quiet, tree-lined street in one of the nicest neighborhoods of St. Paul, Chatsworth is only two blocks from the Minnesota Governor's Mansion on historic Summit Avenue. The wide green lawns and Victorian homes in this area do not seem big-city-like. As one Chatsworth guest wrote, "It's scary for me to go into strange cities alone on business, but I felt so at home here."

CHATSWORTH BED & BREAKFAST, 984 Ashland Avenue, St. Paul, MN 55104; (612) 227-4288. Donna Gustafson, owner-innkeeper. Open all year. Five rooms, 3 with private bath (two with double whirlpool tubs). Rates: $60 to $115, including a healthy continental-plus breakfast. Children usually accepted; no pets; no smoking; no credit cards. Yoga and meditation center on premises. Cafe Latté, Forepaugh's, Lexington, and White Lily recommended for dining. Historic Summit Avenue and Grand Avenue shops are a short walk away. Downtown St. Paul, Ordway Theatre, State Capitol, Science Museum, and several colleges nearby.

DIRECTIONS: from airport take Hwy. 5 north toward St. Paul; turn left at Lexington Pkwy; turn right on Ashland Ave. and proceed 2 blocks to the corner of Ashland and Chatsworth Aves.

1900 DUPONT

Minneapolis at its best

1900 Dupont is one of the prominent homes on Lowry Hill that were built during the nineteenth century for many of Minneapolis' elite. Today, this neighborhood is still the nicest in Minneapolis and about as close to downtown as you can get.

When Chris Viken first moved into the city from neighboring Minnetonka, she was a museum curator looking for a renovation project, not a B&B. But she fell in love with 1900 Dupont and says she "sort of backed into innkeeping." She adds, "I'm surprised I enjoy it as much as I do. The traveler who selects a B&B is a special kind of traveler."

Her dining room and long living room, with its soft green velvet furnishings and grand piano, lend an air of formal elegance. But guests often gravitate instead to the second-floor library with its adjoining solarium. A coved ceiling, stained-glass windows, leather sofas, tiled fireplace, and soft classical music make the library an inviting place to curl up and read.

The three guest rooms are distinguished by iron and brass beds, hardwood floors, and American-oriental rugs. In one bath there is an original claw-foot tub with reproduction brass shower.

Romantic couples who prefer to have their continental breakfast in privacy can roll it into their room on an antique teacart.

Guests love the fact that 1900 Dupont is in such a nice neighborhood, allowing them to leave their car and walk everywhere. It's an easy stroll to Lake of the Isles, where there are wonderful walking paths, canoes and bicycle rentals. The Guthrie Theatre, Walker Art Center, and Sculpture Garden are four blocks away. Best of all—the ice cream shop is just around the corner.

Elliot's Room.

1900 DUPONT, 1900 Dupont Avenue South, Minneapolis, MN 55403; (612) 374-1973; Chris Viken, owner-innkeeper. Open all year. Three rooms, one with private bath and two sharing a bath and a half. Rates: $59 to $85, including continental-plus breakfast. Not appropriate for younger children; no pets; no smoking; no credit cards. Sidney's, 510 Groveland, and Giorgio's recommended for dining nearby. The heart of downtown Minneapolis is one mile away.

DIRECTIONS: from airport follow Hwy. 62 west to Hwy. 35W north to I-94 west. Exit at Hennepin Ave. S. (left); proceed one block to Franklin Ave. and turn right; then turn right at Dupont Ave. S. Inn is 1 block down on the left.

The Library.

The parlor.

EVELO'S B&B

Lit by Tiffany and Handel lamps

Behind the unassuming facade of Evelo's is a treasure chest of splendid woodwork, stained glass, and ornamentation. In fact, this B&B has one of the best preserved Victorian interiors in the Lowry Hill East neighborhood.

The main floor is finished in original, dark oak millwork, lending a rich, Old-World tone to the hallway, parlor, and dining room. Inlaid floors, inset bookshelves, and a built-in buffet are only a sampling of the elaborate detailing found throughout.

Blending in smoothly with this setting are gorgeous Art Nouveau antiques and a remarkable collection of Tiffany and Handel lamps. These colorful lamps are the pride and joy of innkeepers David and Sheryl Evelo.

Different periods of décor mix with exquisite taste here. For example, the stenciled designs on the dining room walls have a definite Moorish look (indeed, they were taken from a pattern that Tiffany fashioned after a Moorish palace in Istanbul) but it balances perfectly with the traditional conservatory look of the dining room.

Up on the third floor, the guest quarters share a bathroom and landing which is supplied with a refrigerator, coffee maker, television, telephone, and magazines. Breakfast—artfully served with sculptured fruit, molded yogurt, pastries, and edible flower garnishes—can be enjoyed on the landing or down in the dining room.

EVELO'S BED & BREAKFAST, 2301 Bryant Avenue South, Minneapolis, MN 55405; (612) 374-9656; Sheryl and David Evelo, owners-innkeepers. Open all year. Three rooms sharing 1½ baths. Rates: $40 single, $50 double, including continental-plus breakfast. Children limited; no pets; no smoking; all credit cards accepted. Lotus, King & I, Loring Cafe, and D'Amico Cucino recommended for dining. Lake of the Isles, Walker Art Center, Guthrie Theater, Minneapolis Institute of Arts, and Uptown shopping within walking distance. Downtown is a 20-minute walk.

DIRECTIONS: from airport, follow "to Minneapolis" signs—55 to Hwy. 62 west to I-35W north towards downtown. Take I-94 west to Hennepin Ave. S. Turn left on Franklin Ave., then right on Bryant Ave. S. Inn is 1½ blocks on left.

A guest room.

Looking towards the front parlor.

LEBLANC HOUSE

A B&B
not to be missed

You can't miss the LeBlanc House, for the colorful gardens and blue-lavender exterior of this turn-of-the-century home are delightfully eye-catching. From April to the first frost, the front yard is a profusion of pink, purple and blue flowers. For the past several years in a row this lovely B&B has won the "Blooming Boulevard" Award of Minneapolis.

Innkeepers Bob Shulstad and Barb Zahasky, the green thumbs behind the gardens, have made the inside of the LeBlanc House equally inviting. Their personal warmth and the attention to detail have turned this into one of the best little B&B's in the Midwest.

The Queen Anne-Dutch Colonial home was constructed in 1897 by William LeBlanc, a Frenchman and builder. Two connecting parlors and the dining room are graced with a beautiful collection of Victorian antiques, including rosewood-and-walnut inlaid chairs, a pump organ, and an old Victrola with push-button record selector.

Stained-glass windows lead you upstairs to the three bedrooms, which are also exquisitely detailed. Zofi's and Amelia's Room feature carved walnut beds and lace-curtained windows with views of downtown Minneapolis. In Marissa's Room there is a round, lace-covered window and enchanting corner of personal heirlooms that spring straight from the pages of *Victoria* Magazine.

LEBLANC HOUSE, 302 University Avenue NE, Minneapolis, MN 55413; (612) 379-2570; Barb Zahasky and Bob Shulstad, owners-innkeepers. Open all year. Three rooms, one with private bath and two with shared bath. Rates: $75 to $95 double, including full breakfast. Children under 12 accepted by arrangement; no pets; smoking allowed only on front porch; all credit cards accepted. Jax Cafe, Yvette's, and many ethnic restaurants recommended for dining. Riverplace, St. Anthony Main, riverboat cruises, and downtown Minneapolis nearby.

DIRECTIONS: from airport, drive west on I-494, then north on I-35W just past downtown Minneapolis. Exit at 4th St. SE and turn left; this leads to University Ave. Turn right on University Ave NE and proceed one block. Inn is on the left.

Marisa's Room.

NEW ORLEANS

A showplace of fine antiques.

JOSEPHINE GUEST HOUSE

The ultimate in New Orleans elegance

Some bed and breakfasts are so outstanding that they become destination points in themselves. Guests don't go there so much for a place to stay as to stay at the place.

This book lists many such establishments; the Josephine Guest House in New Orleans is definitely among them.

The six guest rooms are filled with a charming collection of antiques from both France and Louisiana—a rosewood sofa here, a magnificent carved armoire there; a marquetry day bed upstairs, a rococo gilt mirror downstairs. All the rooms are spacious, with great high ceilings. Some open onto balconies and others onto a gallery that overlooks a private courtyard and surrounding lawns.

Wedgewood china and silver trays comprise the breakfast service, when café au lait, fresh orange juice, and homemade breads and biscuits are served.

The Josephine Guest House is typical of the many fine private homes in New Orleans. A stay here gives the visitor an inside view of a life style that might never be experienced otherwise, apart from having personal friends who live in such a house. Such visitors are indeed fortunate to spend a few days at the Josephine.

THE JOSEPHINE GUEST HOUSE, 1450 Josephine Street, New Orleans, LA 70130; (800) 779-6361, (504) 524-6361; Mary Ann Weilbaecher and Dan Fuselier, owners. Open all year; 6 guest rooms, with private baths and air conditioning. Rates: $75 to $135 double, including continental breakfast of fresh orange juice, café au lait, biscuits. Enquire in advance about children and pets; smoking in public areas; French and a little Spanish spoken; Visa/MasterCard/American Express. Excellent dining nearby at Versailles, Commander's Palace, Caribbean Room.

DIRECTIONS: in the Lower Garden District at the corner of Josephine and Prytania, just off St. Charles Avenue street car line.

The Mallard Suite.

LAMOTHE HOUSE

An opulent town house

A stay at Lamothe House is an experience of a past way of life that is seldom found any more.

Breakfast is served on elegant china and silver in a formal dining room originally used by Jean Lamothe and his family. The furniture is all antique, richly carved and decoratively upholstered with fine fabrics—all of the kind enjoyed by wealthy plantation owners in their opulent New Orleans townhouses.

The two suites that are the jewels of the inn are the Mallard Suite and the Lafayette Suite. The former is named in honor of the famed New Orleans cabinet maker who made most of the room's furniture. The latter is named for the French general, Lafayette, who is depicted in a large ceiling medallion, in remembrance of his friendship to America during the Revolution. The crystal chandeliers, massive canopied beds, Oriental rugs, hand-carved Venetian mirrors, and superb armoires of polished wood that are found throughout the house all call to mind the magnificent way of life for which the Old South was so famous.

The other guest rooms cannot match the splendor of the Mallard and Lafayette suites, but make up for their smaller size by opening onto balconies overlooking the central courtyard, with its abundance of tropical plants, sparkling fountain, and pool.

A few blocks away is the French Quarter, the few historic blocks that have become the most famous in America. Look for Royal Street, with its many shops, and Bourbon Street, with its myriad of Dixieland jazz clubs and its musicians, who still play it like it is.

LAMOTHE HOUSE, 621 Esplanade Avenue, New Orleans, LA 70116; (800) 367-5858, (504) 947-1161; Carol Ann Chauppette, manager. Open all year; 20 guest rooms, with private baths, air conditioning and TV. Rates: $65 to $105 per room. $125 to $205 per suite. Checks required for room deposits. Children welcome; no pets; smoking allowed; Visa/MasterCard/American Express. On the edge of the French Quarter, with close proximity to many restaurants and jazz clubs.

DIRECTIONS: 6 blocks east of Jackson Square, with free parking available.

LAFITTE GUEST HOUSE

Refinement on Bourbon Street

This 1848, three-story family home was one of the most expensive buildings put up in the Vieux Carré district of New Orleans before the Civil War. It has now been magnificently restored as a bed and breakfast.

New Orleans, sitting at the end of the Mississippi's long trek through America's heartland, was the major social and business center of the South, attracting both the rich and the infamous. Old movies give a glimpse into the life of that time, and color our imaginations, but the opportunity to stay at one of the homes original to that glittering period is the icing on the fabulous cake that was New Orleans.

The Guyton family felt privileged in 1980 when it had the opportunity to acquire the Lafitte house. Since 1952 it had been functioning under that name as a guest house, with varying success. They immediately began restoration, to return the house to its original grandeur.

Now guests can live, for a few days, in a grand house, full of fine antiques and excellent reproductions from around the world. The house is just as it would have been in the old days, when ships brought the world's booty to New Orleans' harbors for the enjoyment of the townspeople. Eclectic furnishings were unavoidable, given the wide choice they had. Combined with this, of course, are all the modern conveniences guests could wish for.

Right outside the door are the wonders of the French Quarter, New Orleans most famous district. There, real streetcars bring people from other areas to mingle with those fortunate enough to be staying right in the heart of the French Quarter. Together they flock to the clubs to hear the original Dixieland jazz that spread from here throughout the nation. And here they enjoy the finest restaurants outside of Paris, with liberal adaptation to local flavors.

LAFITTE GUEST HOUSE, 1003 Bourbon Street, New Orleans, LA 70116; (800) 331-7971, (504) 581-2678; John Maher, manager. Open all year; 14 guest rooms, with private baths. Rates: $59 to $165 per room, including continental breakfast. Children welcome; no pets; smoking allowed; Visa/MasterCard/American Express/Discover. In heart of French Quarter near all its restaurants, jazz clubs.

DIRECTIONS: Bourbon Street is one of the most famous in the French Quarter; off-street parking at inn $5 extra.

ALL PHOTOGRAPHS BY ALAN KARCHMER

A spacious penthouse suite.

SONIAT HOUSE

In the heart of the French Quarter

This wonderful, small bed and breakfast hotel in the heart of New Orleans' French Quarter totally reflects the discriminating taste of its owners, Rodney and Frances Smith.

Inveterate collectors with a taste for travel, they accumulated a fine collection of English and French antiques over twenty-five years. To this they have added a number of local Louisiana pieces and a collection of hand carved, four-poster beds made especially for the hotel by a local craftsman. Add to this a collection of lush Oriental rugs and another collection of modern prints, drawings, and paintings spread throughout the rooms, and you will have an idea of the furnishings that comprise this elegant, historic townhouse built in 1829 by a prosperous plantation owner, Joseph Soniat Duffosat.

Although all the rooms are different, they have a number of details in common: soft down pillows, fine cotton bed linens, bathside telephones, and especially aromatic soaps. A breakfast of hot biscuits, homemade preserves, and Creole coffee, is served in your room or in the lounge.

The lounge, by the way, has a private honor bar for guests who like to mix their own drinks. For the rest of the time, there is the famous French Quarter with its multitude of restaurants and jazz clubs.

SONIAT HOUSE, 1133 Chartres Street, New Orleans, LA 70116; (800) 544-8808; Rodney Smith, owner-manager. Open all year: 24 guest rooms and suites, with private baths. Rates: $135 to $185, $225 semi-suites, $350 master suites, all double occupancy; southern continental breakfast $5 extra. French and Spanish spoken; Visa/MasterCard/American Express. 24 hour concierge for advice and help with dining and reservations. Designated as a Historic Hotel of America by the National Trust.

DIRECTIONS: in heart of French Quarter 3 blocks from Jackson Square.

NEW YORK

The Spa Suite spa.

· INN NEW YORK CITY

Inn-credible

When German *Vogue* touted New York City accommodations in their April, 1993 issue, they mentioned only two: The Ritz Carlton and Inn New York City.

Located on the upper West side, the Inn New York City is a beautifully-pampered brownstone that has been transformed into an artwork by a mother and her daughter. Ruth Mensch, an interior decorator and her daughter, Elyn, a fabric designer, have combined their formidable talents to create a fantasy Victorian world with interiors that are both romantic and dramatic.

The result is four incredible suites. The first floor Parlor Suite, over fifty feet in length, has its own terrace. A king-sized bed with stained-glass headboard and an antique quilt faces a woodburning fireplace. In the center of the room, a Baldwin spinet piano leads to a couch, side chairs, and raised platform for dining. The entire space is abloom with rose-adorned fabrics and carpeting.

The second floor Spa Suite is covered in blues, soft and romantic. A built-in king-sized bed sits on a stepped oak platform. Built-in armoires, a lady's desk, a soft easy chair, and fireplace are just the beginning. In another room, an oversized uniquely decorated spa overwhelms: a generous double Jacuzzi, a sauna, bidet, genuine old barberchair, and a wall cabinet artfully filled with Victorian dolls and bric-a-brac complete the scene.

Two suites, The Vermont, on the ground floor, with a country house feeling and a private entrance, and The Loft Suite, on the third floor, with a fourteen-foot beamed ceiling and sponge-painted guestroom with leaded stained-glass skylight, are captivating.

All of the suites have refrigerators stocked with delicacies from Zabar's and other legendary food palaces. Individual needs are catered to and guests feel like royalty.

INN NEW YORK CITY, (212) 580-1900; Elyn and Ruth Mensch, owners. Open all year. Four suites with private baths, 2 with Jacuzzis. Rates: $175 to $240 per suite, including breakfast. Not suitable for children; no pets; no smoking; Visa/MasterCard/American Express. Near Lincoln Center and Sunday flea market, and limitless choice of restaurants.

DIRECTIONS: off Broadway on Upper West Side. Address provided

GEORGE W. GARDNER

NYC—GRAMERCY PARK

Historical comfort

Between Gramercy and Stuyvesant Parks, in an old landmark building that traces its history back to Peter Stuyvesant, this triplex bed and breakfast is pure delight. The streets surrounding it have been well walked by the famous figures who have lived here, such as Mark Twain, O. Henry, Anton Dvorak, and Samuel Tilden.

Shaded and draped in paisley, the oak floored parlor has sofas piled high with Persian printed pillows. A Victorian china cupboard, drop leaf desk, silver tea service, and an old railroad clock add interest and warmth. Breakfast is served at a round oak table under a floral crystal drop chandelier.

Whether you are nestled in the bright Mexican-yellow room with pink accents on the lowest level or two flights up in the space with skylighted gallery and access to the geranium-potted deck, you will be pleased with your surroundings.

The hostess, who is native to Manhattan, will knowledgably direct you, depending upon your interests. There is a constant blossoming of trendy restaurants in this newly energized area as well as the old standbys like Pete's Tavern, Sal Anthony's, Fat Tuesdays, and the Gramercy Park Hotel.

GRAMERCY PARK. Landmark brownstone building. Open year-round. Two guest rooms with shared bath. Rates: $65 single, $80 double. Expanded continental breakfast included. Children welcome; no pets; smoking permitted; MasterCard/Visa/American Express. Near to Gramercy Park, Greenwich Village, midtown. *Represented by Urban Ventures, Inc., New York City.* (212) 594-5650.

NYC—GREENWICH VILLAGE

Sophisticated décor

The airy cheerful apartment has two guestrooms: a pretty floral bedroom/sitting room with Eastlake chest and mirror, where you can sit up in bed and survey Bleecker Street, and a den with high-riser, shelves of books, a desk, and typewriter. Art work covers all the walls—movie posters, two surprisingly striking vintage Red Cross posters, and botanicals. A varied selection of greenery and a colorfully patterned rug add to the charm and warmth.

The hosts are so well liked that guests have been known to throw parties for them before leaving for home. An entry in the guest book reads: "I have a new home in a big city. I will never be lonely again."

GREENWICH VILLAGE. Modern high rise building with views of lower Broadway. Open year-round. Two guest rooms, with a shared bath. Rates: $65 single, $80 double. Continental breakfast included. Children over six welcome; no pets; smoking permitted; MasterCard/Visa/American Express. Close to Chinatown, Little Italy, Washington Square Park, Soho. *Represented by Urban Ventures, Inc., New York City.* (212) 594-5650.

GEORGE W. GARDNER

GEORGE W. GARDNER

NYC—UPPER WEST SIDE

Spacious brownstone in a dynamic area

A sense of spaciousness comes from the fact that this three-story brownstone townhouse is a single-family dwelling. The third floor guest rooms were once the children's bedrooms and retain souvenirs of their adolescence. Just off Columbus Avenue—the most up and coming neighborhood in Manhattan—guests are close to Central Park, the American Museum of Natural History, and Lincoln Center as well as a plethora of fascinating shops and wonderful restaurants.

UPPER WEST SIDE. Brownstone and brick townhouse, built in 1887, with goldfish pond in back yard. Open year-round. Three guest rooms, shared bath. Rates: $55 single, $65 double. Continental breakfast. No children under twelve; no pets; smoking discouraged. Close to Lincoln Center and Columbus Ave. *Represented by Urban Ventures, Inc., New York City.* (212) 594-5650.

Plush and lush.

NYC—SUTTON PLACE

Gilt and elegance

This spacious Sutton Place apartment is furnished as one might expect—*luxuriously.*

Beginning with the marble-floored reception area, the rooms unfold to reveal an elegant décor. A well-polished grand piano, a Scalamandré silk setee, coral-velvet side chairs, a Chinese art deco rug, Louis XVI armchairs, pastoral and floral nineteenth-century oil paintings, and a rosewood game table all command attention. Gilt and elegance are standard fare, and a collection of all-white porcelain china, including Limoges and Wedgewood, is displayed on a coral background.

Two guest rooms, one quite formal and the other furnished in the manner of a den, have private baths appointed with black porcelain and marble fixtures.

A continental breakfast is served each morning by the housekeeper, who will prepare a full breakfast or do your laundry for a small additional fee. All this, plus easy access by taxi to Bloomingdale's, the United Nations, and the Russian Tea Room, makes this location both chic and desirable.

SUTTON PLACE. A luxurious apartment with 2 guest rooms with private baths. Open all year. Rates: $90 for the one guest room, $75 for the other, or $140 for both, including continental breakfast. Children welcome; no pets; smoking allowed; some French spoken; agency accepts Visa/MasterCard/American Express. Directions given upon reservation. Many fine restaurants on nearby 2nd Avenue. *Represented by City Lights Bed & Breakfast Ltd., New York City, (212) 737-7049. Fax (212) 535-2755.*

A richly decorative setting for breakfast.

NYC—GRACIE MANSION AREA

Hob nob with the Mayor

Under the stewardship of a British executive and his charming family, this eclectically-furnished townhouse is just blocks from Gracie Mansion, the home of New York's mayor. It is convenient to the Guggenheim and Metropolitan Museums of Art, and to summer evening concerts overlooking the East River.

A large fireplace dominates the living room and the space resounds with the ambience of a hunting lodge. Add to that a solarium and a rotunda-like dining area with a hanging two-story chandelier, and the effect is completely elegant. English antiques are sprinkled throughout.

The guest rooms are decorated in sensitively coordinated Liberty of London fabrics and wall coverings. Adjoining the rooms is an unusual balcony/library with floor-to-ceiling bookcases and a sumptuous soft leather couch overlooking the rotunda, where breakfast is served.

This upper east side townhouse abounds with good taste.

GRACIE MANSION AREA. A townhouse with 1 guest room and a garden apartment plus another luxurious guest room available occasionally with complimentary French Champagne. Open all year. Rates: $80 guest room, $125 garden apt., $100 special guest room; all include breakfast. Children welcome; no pets; discreet smoking allowed; Spanish, French, some Italian spoken; agency accepts Visa/MasterCard/American Express. Excellent dining in area. *Represented by City Lights Bed & Breakfast Ltd., New York City, (212) 737-7049. Fax (212) 535-2755.*

The Garden Suite.

BEN ASEN

UPPER EAST SIDE

Palatial

Formerly the New Zealand Consulate, this five-story east side townhouse is truly palatial. Complete with a magnificent, imposing staircase and towering crystal chandelier, the formal parlor and dining room are truly grand. The elegant suite on the ground floor is furnished with fine antiques and decorated with choice collectibles. It has access to a lovely garden.

An elevator gently lifts to two elaborately decorated guest rooms on the fifth floor, one with its own terrace overlooking the garden. Purchased in London, wallpapers and fabrics are imaginatively blended. The guest room facing the front of the house has fabric-covered walls and a canopied bed. Every amenity and comfort is provided for.

Breakfast is brought to the room by a housekeeper or may be taken with other guests in a large breakfast room at a round glass table. As one would expect, everything is presented on fine china, set with crystal and silver.

Private dinner parties may be arranged for and there is a special holiday package that includes champagne and holiday gifts.

Bloomingdale's, Tiffany's, Henri Bendel, and Trump Tower are all within blocks.

UPPER EAST SIDE. Two guest rooms with baths and a palatial 1-bedroom suite with bath and kitchen on the garden floor; continental breakfast included, as well as secretarial services and a fax machine. Rates: $170 to $185 per room, $225 suite. Open all year. Inquire about children; no pets; no smoking. Many fine restaurants in immediate area. *Represented by City Lights Bed & Breakfast Ltd.*, P.O. Box 20355 Cherokee Station, New York, NY 10028; (212) 737-7049, FAX (212) 535-2755; Visa/MasterCard/American Express/Diners/Carte Blanche.

DIRECTIONS: given on reservation.

BEN ASEN

PHILADELPHIA

LA RESERVE

A B&B with a French flavor

Built in the 1850's, this four-story townhouse has survived and prospered. Meticulously maintained as a city residence for more than 130 years, it has latterly become a haven for travelers, many from Europe—particularly France.

The parlor is elegant. A candelabra-lit Steinway grand piano of rare vintage awaits your touch. Nearby is a lavishly gilded pier mirror offset by tall silk-draped windows. There are two blue-tufted settees, smartly covered side chairs, and an opulently gilded fireplace, strikingly fanciful, a surprising departure from the staid exterior.

Seven spacious guest rooms, including two generously proportioned suites, have sitting areas, decorative fireplaces, some with bookcases and desks. Three have private baths.

A full breakfast is served in the bay-windowed formal dining room. Offerings vary daily, but always include an egg dish. There is a lovely flower garden

to retire to with a cup of fragrant coffee and the morning paper.

Two blocks from elegant Rittenhouse Square, the inn is just steps away from the Civil War Library and the Rosenbach Museum and Library.

LA RESERVE, 1804 Pine Street, Philadelphia, PA 19103; (800) 354-8401, (215) 735-1137 or 0582; Bill Buchanan, manager. Open all year. Eight rooms, 3 with private baths, 5 sharing. Rates: $40 to $80 per room, including full breakfast. Children welcome; pets on occasion; no smoking preferred; Visa/MasterCard. In Rittenhouse Square area, with lots of first-class restaurants.

DIRECTIONS: south of Rittenhouse Square.

One of the guest rooms.

The sitting room.

THE THOMAS BOND HOUSE

A historical gem

Most Philadelphia buildings are rife with history, and the Thomas Bond House is no exception. Built in 1769 by a physician and surgeon who, with Benjamin Franklin, founded the first public hospital in America, the house is an important example of the classic revival Georgian style of colonial architecture.

Serving as a residence until 1810, the house subsequently had quite a history, functioning as a stocking manufactory, leather tannery, customs brokerage house, and a retail shop, until restored by the National Park Service as a bed and breakfast residence in 1988.

Carefully restored and furnished in the Federal Period, the twelve guest rooms vary from suites on the first floor with queen-sized beds, working fireplaces, and whirlpool baths to two smaller, more simple rooms set in the top-floor pediment.

Weekdays, breakfast is continental, with orange juice and freshly baked muffins. On weekends, however, guest are treated to a sumptuous full breakfast in the formal dining room.

Evenings start with complimentary wine and cheese in front of the working fireplace in the charmingly decorated parlor. Afterwards, the inn-keeper will cheerfully make dinner reservations for guests at any of the many excellent restaurants in the area.

A guest room.

THE THOMAS BOND HOUSE, 129 South 2nd Street, Philadelphia, PA 19106; (800) 845-BOND; Thomas Lantry, managing partner. Open all year. Twelve guest rooms, including 2 suites, all with private baths. Rates: $80 to $150 per room or suite, including continental breakfast on weekdays and full breakfast on weekends. Wine and cheese is served in the evenings before dinner hour. Children welcome; no pets; smoking allowed; Visa/MasterCard/American Express/Diners. On the grounds of Independence National Historic Park with the Liberty Bell, Independence Hall, Congress Hall, U.S. Mint, Betsy Ross House.

DIRECTIONS: downtown Philadelphia near Independence Hall.

INDEPENDENCE PARK INN

Once the showplace of a wealthy merchant

America's older cities abound in elegantly detailed old commercial buildings that are now being appreciated architecturally, and listed by the National Register of Historic Places for their protection.

One particularly fine example is a building in Philadelphia that has special interest because it has been rehabilitated into a luxurious bed and breakfast hotel called the Independence Park Inn. Built in 1856 as a showplace for the wealthy merchant John Elliott, it functioned as his elegant dry goods store in those early days.

Now the building's five stories contain thirty-six high-ceilinged guest rooms. The rooms in front have lovely arched windows that face Independence Park. Furnished with reproduction Chippendale furniture, heavy drapes, prints showing off historic Philadel-

phia, and armoires hiding television sets, the mood created fits perfectly with the historic area in which the inn is situated.

A lavish afternoon tea is served in the lobby, an attractive area with a working fireplace, leather couches, and a large oriental rug.

Just outside, within a few blocks, is a lesson in America's founding history: the Liberty Bell, Independence Mall, the Betsy Ross House, Penn's Landing, Elfreth's Alley, and a reconstruction of Benjamin Franklin's printing shop.

THE INDEPENDENCE PARK INN, 235 Chestnut Street, Philadelphia, PA 19106; (800) 528-1234 [reservations only], (215) 922-4443; Thierry Bompard, manager. Open all year. 36 rooms with private baths and king or queen-sized beds. Rates: *weekdays*, $125 single queen, $135 single king; $135 double queen, $155 double king; *weekends*, $99.50 per room queen, $120 per room king; including continental breakfast. Children welcome; pets acceptable; smoking and non-smoking floors; all major credit cards. Two equipped boardrooms for use of corporate visitors. Nearby to all of Independence Park attractions.

DIRECTIONS: one block from Independence Hall.

A guest room.

A guest room.

SHIPPEN WAY INN

A trio of landmark houses

The Shippen Way Inn is one of Philadelphia's most charming bed and breakfasts. It consists of three landmark houses joined together.

Conveniently linked to the past—near Penn's Landing, Independence Hall, and Benjamin Franklin's Printing Shop—it also borders on South Street, a village within the city, overflowing with trendy restaurants, cafés, galleries, and boutiques.

Nine individually appointed guest rooms include: The Cotswold Room, reminiscent of an English garden; The Blue Room, with a stained-glass window and papered in Laura Ashley; The Quilt Room, furnished in colonial style with handwoven fabrics and quilts; The Rose Room, with a private entrance off the colonial herb and rose garden; and The Four Poster room with a bed so high it requires the use of bed steps.

An elaborate continental breakfast includes home baked breads and fresh fruits. Tea or wine and cheese are served in the afternoon.

A spinning wheel, a cobbler's bench, and other colonial objects are artfully placed throughout. The living room has a fireplace for cozy winter evenings. Carriage rides can be arranged for doing the city in style.

SHIPPEN WAY INN, 416-18 Bainbridge Street, Philadelphia, PA 19147; (800) 245-4873; (215) 627-7266; Ann Foringer and Raymond Rhule, owners. Open all year. Nine rooms with private baths. Rates: $70 to $105 per room, including continental breakfast and afternoon refreshments. Inquire about children; no pets; limited smoking in living room and garden; all major credit cards. Many restaurants nearby on South Street 1 block away.

DIRECTIONS: very near Independence Park, with its historic buildings.

PHOENIX / SCOTTSDALE

The beautiful Thunderbird Room.

WESTWAYS B&B INN

Very luxurious; muchas amenities

The "Private" in Westways Resort is in earnest. When the Spanish Mediterranean home first opened in 1987, it served as a secluded retreat for high-powered corporate executives. Owner Darrell Trapp did everything possible to preserve their sense of privacy, and his Phoenix home still draws many business people and celebrities who are looking for a low-profile, comfortable getaway.

The interior is contemporary with Southwestern accents. A large sunken living room and Arizona room (recreational den) share a fireplace and high vaulted ceilings. Six spacious bedrooms emanate from these common areas. Through the sliding glass doors are a pool, hot tub, fitness room and patio with lounge chairs and complementary towels.

Breakfast, which guests select from a menu, features a different entrée each day, such as Belgian pecan malted waffles or "mucho grande" omelets. Generous munchies—homemade chile, tamales, chicken wings, or ice-cream sundaes—are set out in the afternoon.

Situated in a modern residential area of far-northern Phoenix, Westways appears at first to be rather isolated from the rest of the city. But within a ten-minute drive are two million-dollar sports clubs (one at which Westways guests have membership privileges), three golf courses, and a surprising number of fine restau-rants. Westways also provides mountain bikes for trips to the hilly desert preserve of nearby Thunderbird Park.

If guests opt to stay in for dinner, they can request a "rent-a-chef"—a chef from the Arizona Biltmore, no less—to come over and whip up an intimate gourmet dinner. Taking indulgence one step further, massages can also be arranged at incredibly reasonable prices.

WESTWAYS "PRIVATE" BOUTIQUE RESORT B&B INN, P.O. Box 41624, Phoenix, AZ 85080; (602) 582-3868; Darrell Trapp, innkeeper. Open all year. Six rooms, all with private baths. Rates: $49 to $122, including full breakfast (deluxe continental in summer) and afternoon refreshments. Reservations required at least 24 hours in advance. Catered dinner and massages available at extra charge. Children discouraged; no pets; smoking allowed in restricted areas; Spanish, German, and some French spoken. Visa/MasterCard/American Express. Swimming pool and hot tub on premises. Mountain bikes and country club privileges provided. Surrounded by a desert mountain preserve.

DIRECTIONS: Located in northwest Phoenix in an executive estate area. Directions given upon confirmation.

The back yard pool, patio, and house.

A jewel glowing in the desert darkness.

ARTHUR A. HOLEMAN

INN AT THE CITADEL

Southwestern deluxe

Set in the foothills of Pinnacle Peak, and surrounded by the splendor of the Sonora desert, the Inn at the Citadel offers much more than bed and breakfast. Located atop a small, elegant complex of award-winning restaurants, boutiques, and galleries, the complex wraps around a courtyard, where waterfalls bubble over granite rocks into a pond.

The inn is superb. Eleven luxurious suits are appointed with fireplaces, balconies or terraces, and its contemporary interiors, accented with antique pieces, complement the inn's southwestern style of architecture.

Among the fine restaurants in the complex is *8700 at The Citadel*, featuring unusual southwestern combinations, such as game hen baked in Indian red-rock clay and served with blue-corn stuffing and hazel nut sauce. Another dish, uniquely prepared, is grilled New York steak with wild mushrooms and herb-garlic cheese served on a bed of crispy shoe-string potatoes. Pheasant sausage and roasted Long Island ducking add to the gastronomic extravaganza.

Another restaurant, *The Market*, provides the breakfast for the inn, which guests can either have delivered to their rooms or enjoy at the restaurant. Specialties include freshly baked breads, blue-corn waffles, pastas, salads, burgers, and enchiladas. The Market is the place to be every Thursday evening for the ultimate in outdoor grilling, when fresh salmon, shish kabob, and lobster are served up to the music of the Khani Cole band.

INN AT THE CITADEL, 8700 E. Pinnacle Peak Road, Scottsdale, AZ 85255; (800) 927-8367, (602) 585-6133; Robert and Anita Keyes, owners. Open all year. Eleven rooms and suites with private baths. Rates: $145 to $195 per room or suite, including continental breakfast. Children welcome ($25 extra); small pets acceptable; smoking limited to public areas; Spanish spoken; Visa/MasterCard/American Express/Diners.

DIRECTIONS: call for directions from specific locations.

A guest room.

A bedroom in the guest house.

SCOTTSDALE B&B

A fabulous modern adobe

There is a softness to the Sonoran desert that is nowhere more enhanced than at this fabulous contemporary adobe. Designed by renowned Scottsdale artist William Tull, the seven-thousand-square-foot home is like a sculpted work of art. Walls undulate, rooms flow into one another, and every line is softly curved.

Owner Ramón Vives, a restaurateur originally from Spain, spared no expense on this stunning home which he helped build ten years ago. (Making over two hundred-thousand adobe bricks was one of the no-minor-tasks involved.) Elisa Green, his companion and interior decorator, has blended together a bold ensemble of massive furnishings and striking artwork—paintings, pottery, baskets—from Mexico, Spain and the Southwest. In the living room brightly-colored, overstuffed Guatemalan pillows and throws mingle with sheepskin rugs on black leather couches, while masked Hopi Indians look down from their colorful canvases.

Left, above. *The pool, showing the house on the right and the guest house on the left.* Below. *The living room.*

The décor in every meandering room and alcove is truly exciting.

Palm trees on an immaculate lawn surround the pool. Next to it is a separate, southwestern-style guest house. The pool pavilion features a hi-tech stereo system, large-screen TV, steam sauna, and showers. Another of many artfully concealed TV's is built right into the adobe wall of a tiled, outdoor Jacuzzi. There is also an exercise room, an oversized private tennis court, and no less than nine adobe fireplaces, or *chimeneas*, throughout.

All of the homes in this exclusive Pinnacle Peaks area of northern Scottsdale enjoy ample breathing space. Beyond the electronic gates and low adobe walls is an expanse of quiet, natural desert landscape punctuated by huge cacti and the peaceful sounds of birds and wildlife.

This home must be seen to be believed. It is an extraordinary, luxurious, private retreat.

SCOTTSDALE B & B. Five guest rooms, including 2 separate guest houses with kitchens; all rooms with private baths. Open all year. Rates: $100 to $150, including continental-plus breakfast. Children 10 and over (swimmers only); no pets; smoking outside only; 6 languages spoken. Swimming pool, Jacuzzi, steam room, private tennis court on premises. *Represented by Mi Casa Su Casa*, P.O. Box 950, Tempe, AZ 95280-0950, (800) 456-0682; (602) 990-0682. No credit cards accepted.

DIRECTIONS: in Pinnacle Peak area of Scottsdale. Directions upon confirmation.

MARICOPA MANOR

Join the extended family

Mary Ellen and Paul Kelley obviously enjoy having lots of people at the Manor. After raising twelve children, they further extended their family by opening their home to bed and breakfast guests.

Their 1928 Spanish-style home has an impressive approach, with its curved driveway and graceful archways. To the side is a tranquil courtyard and fountain surrounded by palms, orange trees, and trailing flowers. In the back on the immense lawn, are bird houses, a gazebo spa, and a wonderfully gnarled, sixty-year-old palo verde—the state tree of Arizona.

The formal foyer, embellished with delicate alabaster statues, is flanked by an eighteenth-century French-style living room and music room which contains unusual antique instruments.

Two of the suites are in the main house and three are in separate guest houses on the grounds. Each suite features a different theme, from the ultra-modern Reflections Future to the traditional Victorian Suite. The Library Suite—a favorite of guests—has a comfortable den with desk, TV, phone, and shelves of beautiful leatherbound classics.

MARICOPA MANOR, 15 West Pasadena Avenue, Phoenix, AZ 85013; (602) 274-6302; Mary Ellen and Paul Kelley, owners. Open all year. Five suites, all with private baths; 2 suites in main house; 3 suites in separate guest houses. Rates: $79 to $129, including continental plus breakfast. Children welcome; no pets; smoking allowed in designated areas only; Visa/MasterCard/American Express. A multitude of restaurants nearby, many within walking distance. Hot tub on premises. Golf, tennis, fitness center, and downtown Phoenix nearby.

DIRECTIONS: From I-17, exit at Camelback Rd. and drive east. Turn left on 3rd Ave., then right on Pasadena Ave.

PORTLAND

Stairway to the guest rooms.

HERON HAUS

A little bit of old Hawaii

Perched on the northwest hills of Portland, Julie Keppeler's grand three-story turn-of-the-century house looks out on stunning views of Mount Rainier, Mount St. Helens, and Mount Hood.

Furnished in a classic contemporary style with muted shades, there are touches of antiquity throughout: the family furniture from early days in San Francisco; Indian artifacts, a gift from her stepfather, an authority on the Columbia River Indians; pieces from her mother's unique basket collection; and her own trilobite, ammonite, and brachiopod treasures from her days as a guide at the Natural History Museum in Denver.

Julie Keppeler, the fascinating owner of this bed-and-breakfast inn, lived in Hawaii for twenty-four years, raising her children in a big old plantation house. At the Heron Haus, a wall completely covered with photographs recaptures those days.

Even the guest rooms have Hawaiian names, including Maluhia (peaceful), Manu (bird), and Kulia (Julie's room) named for Julie, the daughter who stripped off four layers of wallpaper before redecorating the room. All of the rooms have ample sitting areas and views of the city and mountains, and two guest suites on the second and third floors

offer baths with special extras. One of the showers with original 1904 plumbing offers seven spray spouts.

Breakfast, which starts with freshly cut fruit, is served in the large dining room that extends across one end of the house. A pastry basket with choice offerings such as fresh pumpkin-raisin and cinnamon-current pastries, date nut rolls, and tangy orange rolls are gathered daily from various baker friends in Portland.

Minutes from downtown Portland, there are neighborhood restaurants offering seven different cuisines, as well as boutiques and specialty shops for browsing.

HERON HAUS BED & BREAKFAST INN, 2545 NW Westover Road, Portland, OR 97210; (503) 274-1846; Julie Keppeler, owner. Five guest rooms and 2 master suites, all with private baths, TVs, sitting areas, and views of the city. Rates: $85 to $145. Includes a generous continental breakfast. Telephone in each room, computer available, swimming pool on premises. Older children welcome; no pets; no smoking; Visa/MasterCard.

DIRECTIONS: from Hwy. 405, take Everett Street exit to Glisan Street. Take left on Glisan to 24th Street (about 10 blocks) and then a left on Johnson Street for 1 block up to Westover Road. Driveway is ½ block up Westover.

WHITE HOUSE

A majestic mansion aptly named

Built in 1910 in what was once a resort area for the Portland elite, this grand house belonged to a rags-to-riches lumber tycoon. The mansion, airy and elegantly proportioned, suited his wife's desire to live in a bright and expansive home instead of a dark Victorian-style house prevalent at the time.

Because it closely resembles the President's home in Washington, D.C., neighbors have aptly nicknamed the 7,600-square-foot mansion the "White House." The colossal classic portico with six Doric columns is reminiscent of southern plantation manors. French arched transoms with amber glass, a second-story curved balustrade balcony, and a Mediterranean red tile roof add contrast to the classic style.

The interior is equally dramatic. Graciously tall windows and twelve-foot-high cove ceilings are trimmed with Honduran mahogany.

Hand-painted wall murals in the building's entrance depict rural scenes which recall the grounds at the turn of the century. The huge living room, dining room, and downstairs ballroom indicate the grand entertaining which took place within their walls.

Inkeepers Larry and Mary Hough handle the grandeur with cheery aplomb. Dublin born, Mary was brought up in an English boardinghouse and takes to hostessing quite naturally. Larry enjoys the challenge of the ongoing restoration and clearly enjoys the guests. Theirs is a happy home where visitors are indulged in luxury and jovial, warm hospitality.

WHITE HOUSE, 1914 N.E. 22nd Avenue, Portland, OR 97212; (503) 287-7131; Larry and Mary Hough, hosts. Six rooms, all with private baths. Rates: $87 to $112. Includes a full breakfast that varies between twelve different English-style menus that may include scones, soda bread, oatmeal, and cooked fruits. Children discouraged; no pets; no smoking; Visa/MasterCard. Seven minutes from downtown business district.

DIRECTIONS: from the north on I-5, take the Coliseum exit. Proceed straight and make a left onto Weildler Blvd. Go to 22nd Ave. and turn left. From the south on I-5, take a right onto Weildler Blvd. Go to 22nd Ave. and turn left.

Above, the two-story Doric columns dominate the entrance.

MacMASTER HOUSE

Decorated with flair

MacMaster House, with its wonderful high-ceilinged rooms, is one of Portland's more unusual bed and breakfasts, the inspiration being the eclectic tastes of its owner, Cecilia Murphy. After a lengthy career in Oregon radio broadcasting, Cecilia directed her talents to innkeeping in 1986, and has decorated the inn with flair and imagination.

Cecilia attributes her "Out of Africa" period to the dramatic wall mural in the MacMaster suite, depicting zebras galloping across a sun-drenched plain dotted by distant acacia trees. A bamboo four-poster bed, draped with vibrant cotton, and an animal hide throw carpet, adds to the exotic theme. These blend splendidly with the room's classic features such as a gilt-edged mirror over the fireplace, and wonderful antique armchairs. A talented artist, and friend of Cecilia's, has carried the same unique combination of drama, elegance, and whimsy into three other guest rooms, with wall-painting 'headboards' depicting a carousel horse, delicate ferns, and a brilliantly-colored peacock.

A gracious dining room with fireplace, Chinese Chippendale chairs, intricately-carved camphor chest, and a beautifully hand-painted Egyptian geese panel, sets the scene for the guests' breakfast. Fruit juice is accompanied by artistically-presented seasonal fruit, and delicious homemade muffins. Wonderfully creative cooking is produced by Cecilia's kitchen staff, with entrées revolving around regional themes such as Cajun and Southwest cuisine. The food, ambience, and charming, attentive innkeeper make MacMaster House a very special place.

MAC MASTER HOUSE, 1041 S.W. Vista Avenue, Portland, OR 97205; (503) 223-7362. Cecilia Murphy, owner. Open all year. Five guest rooms, all with TV; 4 with fireplaces and queen beds; 2 rooms have private baths; 3 rooms share 1½ baths. Rates: $75 to $110, including full gourmet breakfast. Children over 14 welcome; no pets; no smoking inside; Visa/MasterCard/American Express. Magnificent Washington Park, boutiques, galleries and several premier restaurants within walking distance.

DIRECTIONS: *from the north:* take I-405 south off I-5 and exit at Burnside; turn right on Burnside and watch for the Volvo sign on the left; turn left on St. Clair just after the Volvo dealership; turn right on Park Place; go 1 block to Vista and turn left at the light; see Mac Master House on the right. *From the south:* take I-405 north off I-5 and follow to Salmon St. exit; turn left on Taylor and continue to 18th; turn left on 18th and go 1 block; turn right on Salmon; follow Scenic Route signs as Salmon turns into Park Place; turn left at light on Vista and watch for Mac Master House on the right.

ST. LOUIS

Sarah and Kendall Winter.

The parlor pianist, Jay Epstein, accompanies breakfast.

THE WINTER HOUSE

Victorian décor

This red-brick, three-story Victorian home was built in 1897 just before the St. Louis World's Fair. Painstakingly restored by owners Sarah and Kendall Winter, the house is highlighted by embossed, hand-painted French panels in the parlor, a pressed tin ceiling in the bedroom, and old-fashioned Victorian décor throughout.

Down a private hallway on the main level is the Carrie Kimbrell Room, in soft peach tones. Spacious and high-ceilinged, the room features a vanity table, old-fashioned writing desk, and pineapple-poster bed. Upstairs, the two-bedroom Alma Culp Suite boasts an original coal-burning fireplace, balcony, and sitting room.

The Winters, both thirty-year residents of St. Louis, are attentive, gracious hosts. They provide their guests with lots of extras, including a fruit basket, fine chocolates, afternoon refreshments, fresh flowers, nice toiletries, and an intercom line to the innkeepers.

In the morning, by advance request, classical pianist Jay Epstein will serenade guests in the parlor while breakfast is served on antique Wedgewood china in the adjoining dining room. Breakfast starts with fresh-squeezed orange juice and includes a baked apple or pear, various breads, and perhaps one of Kendall's oven-baked pancakes. A fire warms the parlor in cold weather.

From the B&B it is a pleasant walk through Tower Grove Park to the Missouri Botanical Garden (also known as Shaw's Garden), one of the nation's oldest gardens. Grand Boulevard, just around the corner, offers an international shopping district with many ethnic restaurants.

THE WINTER HOUSE, 3522 Arsenal Street, St. Louis, MO 63118; (314) 664-4399; Sarah and Kendall Winter, owners-innkeepers. Closed Christmas week. One bedroom plus a suite accommodating 4, both with private baths. Rates: $55 to $75, including continental plus breakfast. Children accepted; no pets; no smoking; all credit cards accepted. Cafe de Manila and St. Louis Bread Co. recommended for dining. Tower Grove Park, Missouri Botanical Garden, tennis courts, Anheuser Busch Brewery, Fox theater, and downtown nearby.

DIRECTIONS: from I-44 take exit 288 south on Grand Blvd. for 1 mile; turn left on Arsenal St. From I-64 (State 40) exit at Grand Blvd. Proceed south 2 miles and turn left on Arsenal St. Inn is on the right.

A fine old stairway.

EASTLAKE INN

A suburban setting

Lori and Dan Ashdown spent ten years searching for the perfect town, nicest neighborhood, and most ideal home in which to open a B&B. They found it in Kirkwood, a lovely outer suburb of St. Louis. This tidy little town with its main street of antiques shops and boutiques is also aptly called "Green Tree City, U.S.A." There are so many trees here that it's hard to believe the city is only twenty minutes away.

A 1920's colonial home, the Eastlake Inn faces a wide green lawn surrounded by tall dogwoods, catalpa trees, bald cypress, and American holly bushes. One guest room is named after the magnolia tree which blooms seasonally outside the window. The Garden Room overlooks the perennial garden. The inn and grounds provide a tranquil setting for intimate weddings.

Highlighting the fresh, cheerful home are lovely, turn-of-the-century furnishings designed by Charles Eastlake. Dried wreaths, made by Lori, trim the walls. Congregated in the cozy, Americana-style living room are Lori's collection of antique dolls, bears, and an English chess set complete with Norman and Saxon chessmen.

Breakfast is served either in the dining room, which is crowned by a 1,170-piece Portuguese chandelier, or out on the sun porch when weather permits. The breakfast menu includes such fare as oven-baked French toast, fresh fruit from the local farmer's market, whole wheat pancakes, omelets, and homemade breads.

Lori, a native of St. Louis and member of the Kirkwood Chamber of Commerce, will gladly share her knowledge of the area. Her B&B is perfect for

Dining Room.

people who want a clean, small-town atmosphere within easy access to the city. Downtown St. Louis is close by . . . but you might end up never leaving Kirkwood!

THE EASTLAKE INN BED & BREAKFAST, 703 North Kirkwood Road, St. Louis, MO 63122; (314) 965-0066; (314) 771-1993 (*River Country B&B Reservation Service*); Lori and Dan Ashdown, owners-innkeepers. Open all year. Three rooms, each with private bath. Rates: $55 to $70, including full breakfast. No children under 10 years; no pets; no smoking; Visa/MasterCard. Ikemeiers, Caliente, Mike Duffy's, and Schneidhorst's recommended for dining. Kirkwood Park, Kirkwood antique shops, and the Magic House nearby. Carriage rides from the inn can be arranged.

DIRECTIONS: Inn is located in Kirkwood, between I-44 and I-64. From I-270 exit at Manchester Rd. Proceed east for 2 miles and turn right on Kirkwood Rd.; drive south 5 blocks to the corner of West Jewel and Kirkwood Rd. Inn is on the right. Amtrak also stops in Kirkwood.

Living Room.

Magnolia Room.

A guest room.

THE ANTIQUE SHOP B&B

Sleeping with antiques

This 1904 building consists of an antique co-op downstairs and a B&B upstairs. Richard Cottrell, one of the antique dealers, recently converted the three-bedroom upstairs apartment into a self-catered bed and breakfast.

As Richard points out, his B&B is very casual and not for guests who like to have everything done for them. He greets you from his shop and will provide a continental breakfast upon request. But there are so many charming cafés in the area that many guests opt to have their breakfast out instead. The surrounding West End neighborhood is one of the nicest pockets of urban St. Louis, loaded with wonderful antiques shops, art galleries, outdoor cafés, and pubs.

THE ANTIQUE SHOP BED & BREAKFAST, 4732 McPherson, St. Louis, MO 63108; (314) 771-1993 (*River Country B&B Reservation Service*); Richard Cottrell and Mary Ann Kovac, hosts. Open all year. Three bedrooms, each with private bath, common room with television, kitchen and sun room. Rates: $50 to $75, including self-serve continental breakfast. Children accepted; pets accepted; Visa/MasterCard.

DIRECTIONS: from I-64 exit at Kingshighway Blvd; drive north to McPherson and turn right. From I-70 exit at Kingshighway Blvd; drive south to McPherson and turn left. B&B is above West End Gallery and Antiques Shop; look for the hosts in the shop.

The antiques shop, with the B & B above.

LAFAYETTE HOUSE

Lots of collectibles

Built in 1876, this red-brick Queen Anne mansion which overlooks Lafayette Park is the closest B&B to downtown St. Louis. For the past decade, innkeepers Sarah and Jack Milligan have been providing their guests with warm, homey, happily-cluttered surroundings that are literally just like a stay at grandma's.

Every wall and counter of the downstairs living room, dining room and kitchen are overflowing with The Milligan's lifetime collection of teapots, milk glass, kitchen molds, angels, bells, cat prints, and china. As for the books—Sarah has over two thousand cookbooks alone.

A lovable and helpful innkeeper, Sarah spends every Thursday baking such breakfast treats as peanut butter bread and banana-chocolate chip bread. Her hearty, country-style breakfasts might also include potato pancakes, eggs, and bacon or sausage, fueling guests for a full day of sightseeing.

LAFAYETTE HOUSE, 2156 Lafayette Avenue, St. Louis, MO 63104; (314) 772-4429; Sarah and Jack Milligan, owners-innkeepers. Open all year. Four rooms, including one suite with kitchen; private and shared baths. Rates: $45 to $75, including full breakfast and refreshments. Airport/station pickups extra charge. Children welcome; no pets; smoking limited to lounge only; Visa/MasterCard.

DIRECTIONS: from I-44 exit at Jefferson Ave; proceed north 1 block and turn right on Lafayette Ave.

A guest room.

SALT LAKE CITY

Jan Bartlett and Nancy Saxton, innkeepers.

SALTAIR BED & BREAKFAST

Bed down with Amish quilts

A guest room.

Nancy Saxton and Jan Bartlett are the innkeepers at this historic 1903 bed and breakfast, and their taste and discrimination are evident throughout.

Each of the four guest rooms has a different color scheme coordinated with the beautiful Amish quilts that decorate the brass beds. The fifth room has an oak bed, fluffy lace curtains, and delicately flowered wallpaper.

In the dining room, with its sturdy oak table, guests are seated in a handsome set of turn-of-the-century oak chairs to partake of an ample breakfast. An exotic blend of fruit juice and yogurt is the first course, followed by a choice of delicious waffles, French toast, or pancakes with syrup.

Old photographs and posters on the walls explain the inn's name: Saltair. They show Saltair resort as it was in the old days when it was a great attraction on the beach at the Great Salt Lake. One hundred years later it has been rebuilt and you can go there again, if only to enjoy a dip in the lake.

Current attractions of Salt Lake City are within a short distance from the inn: the famous Temple and Square that everyone wants to see; Symphony Hall; the Utah State Capital; the Family History Library of Genealogy, where anyone can trace the lineage of their family.

SALTAIR BED AND BREAKFAST, 164 South 900 East, Salt Lake City, UT 84102; (800) 733-8184; Jan Bartlett and Nancy Saxton, innkeepers. Open all year. Five rooms, 3 with shared baths, 2 with private baths; Alpine Cottage sleeps 4. Rates: $34 to $79 per room; cottage $79 to $110. Includes full breakfast. Well-behaved children welcome—those under 8 stay in cottage only; no pets; no smoking; Visa/American Express/MasterCard/Discover Card. Cottage particularly suited to parties of skiers in wintertime.

DIRECTIONS: off South Temple Street in the direction of the University of Utah.

The Oriental Suite.

PINE CREST B&B INN

In one word— *stunning*

Built in 1915 of natural stone and richly finished wood paneling by the local quarry owner, Pinecrest was one of the most luxurious homes in Utah. Situated on six acres of landscaped gardens, streams, and ponds, it is now one of Utah's most stunning bed and breakfasts, with four superbly furnished guest rooms in the main house and two separate guest cabins suitable for families.

Hosts Phil and Donnetta Davis envisaged a bed and breakfast inn when they discovered the estate for sale eight years ago. Because the house was in immaculate condition, they could concentrate their creative efforts on furnishing the rooms to suit their own exquisite tastes.

The results are four sumptuous guest rooms:

The Oriental Suite, finished in cherrywood paneling, with antique Chinese furniture, a rose-colored Jacuzzi, and a king-sized bed.

Left, above. The library. Below. The dining room.

The English Library Room, with a king-sized bed, a marble tub, and a balcony overlooking a stream;

The Jamaican Jacuzzi Room, with a sunken tub, a sauna, a king-sized bed, and a private entrance;

The Holland Blue Room, which looks exactly like it sounds, with white wicker furniture and a queen-sized bed.

A full breakfast of banana sour cream pancakes or crêpes is served in the dining room overlooking the gardens, or on the deck by the stream.

Twenty minutes drive from downtown Salt Lake City, the inn is situated in Emigration Canyon, the route the Mormons first used to find their way into Salt Lake Valley, where they settled. Nearby are two fine restaurants, a popular diner, and the city's zoo.

We should warn you, however: this place is so enchanting that you won't want to leave.

PINECREST BED & BREAKFAST INN, 6211 Emigration Canyon Road, Salt Lake City, UT 84108; (801) 583-6663; Phil and Donnetta Davis, owners. Open all year. 6 guest rooms and suites with private baths. Rates $70 to $175 per room, including full breakfast. Children 10 and over welcome; no pets; no smoking; Visa/MasterCard/American Express.

DIRECTIONS: detailed instructions on reservation.

Room 7.

BRIGHAM STREET INN

Designers' showcase

If Bloomingdales owned an inn, this would be it. It is the showplace of the West, an elegant bed and breakfast abounding in works of art and rooms that feature a dozen designers' concepts.

Innkeeper Nancy Pace came upon the house when she chaired the Utah Heritage Foundation's *Designers Showcase* in 1982. Utah's leading designers were asked to decorate the rooms, and have created a stunning set of diverse and beautiful interiors.

The foyer's original oak wainscoting and staircase and the birds-eye maple fireplace in the parlor are merely a beginning. The old Tibetan tapestry in the formal dining room and the horsehair porter's chair and Steinway grand in the parlor add unanticipated drama, while upstairs each guest room vies for attention. Victorian revival, American Federal, classic eighteenth century, country, Oriental, and Art Nouveau (circa Hector Guimard) are all periods on display. The "cellar space" is modern casual elegance—a town house suite with living room, bedroom, kitchen, double whirlpool bath, and pri-

Left, above. The elegant dining room, where breakfast is served. Below. Room 4.

vate garden entrance.

After restoration, furnishing, and the fund raising event were over, Nancy was so taken with the house that she bought it and became a bona fide innkeeper. No one is more qualified. Concerned with both quality and attention to detail, she welcomes business people, summer tourists, and winter skiers with equal hospitality, and almost anything can be arranged by the caring and capable staff.

BRIGHAM STREET INN, 1135 East South Temple Street, Salt Lake City, UT 84102; (801) 364-4461; Fax (801) 521-3201; Nancy Pace, innkeeper. Open all year. Nine rooms, including 1 suite, all with private baths. Rates: $75 to $115 per room, suite $150, including continental breakfast. Children welcome; no pets; Visa/MasterCard/American Express/Discover Card. Prime ski areas at Snowbird and Alta 45 minutes away.

DIRECTIONS: South Temple St. runs east from the Temple.

SAN ANTONIO

THE OGÉ HOUSE

European elegance

Showcased as one of San Antonio's most beautiful bed and breakfast establishments, the Ogé House is set on the banks of the San Antonio River. A spectacular Greek Revival mansion, it is a jewel on the River Walk, displayed on an acre-and-a-half of carefully manicured greenery. The three-story dwelling is appointed with spacious verandas on each of its three floors.

Built in 1857, the house was once owned by Texas ranger, cattle rancher, and businessman Louis Ogé. Today is it managed in the style of an exquisite small European inn, with a feeling of intimacy and an attentiveness to personal detail. Five beautifully decorated rooms and five gracious suites with fireplaces and king-sized beds are furnished with antiques, oriental carpets, and well-chosen artworks. There is a grand foyer and an inviting library and everything is bathed in a romantic glow.

Breakfast is served in the opulent formal dining

Left. The beautifully decorated hallway and staircase.

room with its antique Chippendale-style chairs and burgundy-covered private tables bedecked with lace and fresh flowers. The deluxe continental breakfast, including twelve breads and pastries, is served on Wedgewood china, crystal, and silver.

THE OGÉ HOUSE, 209 Washington Street, San Antonio, TX 78204; (800) 242-2770, (210) 223-2353, FAX (210) 226-5812; Patrick and Sharrie Magatagan. Open all year. Five rooms and 4 suites, all with private baths. Rates: (weekends) $125 to $135 per room, $165 to $195 per suite, including deluxe continental breakfast; lower rates Mon. to Thur. Children over 16 welcome; no pets; smoking on veranda only; a little Spanish spoken; Visa/MasterCard/American Express. Three blocks from 70 restaurants. River Walk nearby.

DIRECTIONS: 3½ blocks south of Alamo Street Convention Center.

The Persian Suite describes this guest room perfectly.

FALLING PINES B&B INN

And then there's the Persian Suite

Now, *this* is a mansion. Situated in San Antonio's historic Monte Verde District, Falling Pines encompasses an entire residential block. Built in 1911, the magnificent brick and limestone mansion is distinguished by Italianate archways, abundant balconies, and pine trees towering in front.

The nine-thousand-square-foot interior is even more palatial. Quarter-cut oak paneling, Oriental carpets, and luxurious furnishings on the ground floor exude the somber grandeur of a baronial manor. In the music room is an 1860 Steinway piano; in the living room are luxurious silk couches; in the dining room are high, carved chairs. There is also a library and tiled solarium where breakfast is served.

Owner Bob Daubert, an oil businessman, and his wife Grace have artfully embellished the three second-floor guest rooms. One room contains a seventeenth-century English cherry-wood sleigh bed. Another carries a masculine theme, while the third is serenely appointed in shades of cream.

But the crowning glory of Falling Pines is the Persian Suite on the third floor. What was formerly the attic ballroom has been transformed into a contemporary version of "Arabian Nights." Hundreds of yards of beige artist's canvas have been gathered and draped from every wall and ceiling, creating the effect of an enormous tent. A cream-colored bed seems to float out from the center, as does the free-standing shower in the bathroom (which, by the way, is a most remarkable bathroom). The all-neutral tones of cream, beige and brown throughout the suite are most striking. From one of its two balconies are views of downtown San Antonio.

In every room there are flowers and a decanter of brandy with cut crystal glasses. The full breakfast includes Bob's homemade strudel.

FALLING PINES B&B INN, 300 West French Place, San Antonio, TX 78212; (800) 880-4580; (210) 733-1998; Grace and Bob Daubert, owners. Open all year. Four rooms, including one suite; all rooms with private baths. Rates: $87 to $130.50, including full breakfast. Children over 10 accepted; no pets; no smoking; Spanish spoken. Visa/MasterCard/American Express. La Fonda and Paisano's recommended for dining. Guest memberships at country club included. San Pedro Park, San Antonio Zoo, and tennis center nearby.

DIRECTIONS: From US 281 (also called I-37), exit at Mulberry St. and drive west. Turn left on Belknap and follow to W. French Pl. Inn is large mansion on Belknap and French Pl.

BECKMANN INN

A wedding gift for a miller's daughter

Perfectly located for enjoying San Antonio at its very best, the Beckmann Inn is situated right across from where the River Walk begins. A wedding gift for the daughter of the Guenther flour mill family, the house was built at the turn of the century on the mill grounds.

A beautiful wrap-around porch encircles the house, extending from Madison Street around to Guenther Street creating a new address that was different from that of a famous brothel in the neighborhood. The wicker furniture on the porch is inviting to new arrivals, who are greeted with a "welcoming cup of tea."

Betty Jo Beckmann always admired the house when she visited San Antonio, and so when she purchased it, it was a dream come true. Originally built in Victorian style, the house has been plied with Greek Revival elements to befit the fashion of a later day.

Convinced that *the beds* and *the breakfasts* were the most important elements in this new-for-them-venture, the Beckmanns scoured four mid-west states for special beds. Now residing in five different guest rooms, the unusual beds include one that is a museum-quality nine-foot chestnut queen-sized Victorian.

Other notables include the Library Room, with its rare burled pine mantel and the dining rooms' large beveled-glass window overlooking the white wicker-furnished sun porch. The accommodations in the Carriage House look out on flower beds and a garden fountain.

Breakfasts are served on china, complete with crystal and silver. Offerings include cranberry-glazed pears, stuffed French toast with apricot glaze, and Canadian bacon. A unique part of breakfast are the luscious desserts.

A guest room.

BECKMANN INN AND CARRIAGE HOUSE, 222 East Guenther Street, San Antonio, TX 78204; (210) 229-1449; Betty Jo and Don Schwartz, owners. Open all year. Five guest rooms with private baths. Rates: $80 to $120 per room, including full breakfast. Children over 12 welcome; no pets; no smoking; Visa/MasterCard/American Express/ Diners.

DIRECTIONS: in Southtown, off South Alamo.

Central Hall and parlor.

TERRELL CASTLE B&B

British décor

While Edwin Terrell served as the American ambassador to Belgium in the 1890s, he was enthralled by the romantic castles of Europe. When Terrell returned home to Texas he commissioned a British architect to design a "castle for his bride" and their six children.

When Katherine Poulis and her daughter, Nancy Haley, bought the Castle in 1986, it had been turned into apartments and was in a sorry state. They spent months restoring it to its former grandeur.

The downstairs common areas are elegantly appointed with Victorian antiques from Katherine and Nancy's previous homes. In the central hall is a unique "coffin niche" with a fireplace, while an impressive white staircase sweeps above it. The fine parquet floors are covered with Oriental carpets. The parlor, library, and dining room also emanate from the central hall.

The guest quarters, most with British décor, meander all over the upper floors, with multiple hallways and stairs. Several rooms are large enough to accommodate families. The Terrell Suite is a popular choice, featuring a large bay window, fireplace, and its own sun room.

Breakfast can be had in the dining room at absolutely any time of the morning. (No kidding—from 7:30 to noon!) Huge bowls of fruit are served, along with tasty muffins and biscuits, eggs, sausage, and bacon. Then it's time to head to downtown San Antonio for a River Walk or tour of the Alamo.

TERRELL CASTLE BED AND BREAKFAST, 950 East Grayson Street, San Antonio, TX 78208; (800) 356-1605; (210) 271-9145; Nancy Jane Haley and Katherine M. Poulis, owners. Open all year. Nine rooms and suites; 7 rooms with private baths, 2 sharing a bath; some rooms with fireplaces. Rates: $70 to $85, single; $85 to $100, double; extra person $15 (no charge for children 6 and under); includes full breakfast. Children accepted; pets accepted; smoking allowed; Spanish spoken. Visa/MasterCard/American Express/Discover. About 20 blocks to the Alamo and River Walk.

DIRECTIONS: From US 281 (also called I-37) south, exit at Josephine-Grayson Sts. and turn left on Grayson. Inn is 6 blocks down on right.

The Tower Suite.

SAN DIEGO

The extraordinary Victorian parlor.

HERITAGE PARK B&B INN

In the heart of Old Town

The most historic part of San Diego, popularly known as Old Town, was claimed for the King of Spain in 1769. Old Town's famous Presidio Park Plaza, Adobe Chapel, and other historic buildings are adjacent to a seven-acre hillside preserve called Heritage Park Victorian Village. Numerous Victorian houses were moved here when threatened with demolition.

One of the preserved homes, now Heritage Park Bed and Breakfast Inn, was literally cut in half and rejoined at its present site. It is an 1889 Queen Anne, characterized by a two-story corner tower, encircling veranda, and gingerbread fretwork.

The interior is filled with redwood trim, stained glass, and gaslight fixtures. The décor is very Victorian, with oriental rugs over wood floors, claw-foot tubs, and old-fashioned wall coverings.

Owners Charles and Nancy Helsper, thirty-year residents of San Diego, keep their guests amply fed with a full breakfast each morning,

HERITAGE PARK BED & BREAKFAST INN, 2470 Heritage Park Row, San Diego, CA 92110; (619) 299-6832; (800) 995-2470; Nancy and Charles Helsper, owners. Open all year. Eight rooms, four with private bath; one two-bedroom suite. Rates: $80 to $135, including full breakfast. Midweek business packages available. Children accepted; no pets; smoking allowed on the veranda; handicapped access; Spanish spoken; MasterCard/Visa.

DIRECTIONS: from downtown and airport: I-5 north to Old Town Avenue off-ramp. Left on Old Town Avenue, right on Harney to Heritage Park. From LA: I-5 south to Old Town Avenue off-ramp. Left on San Diego Avenue and right on Harney.

The Belle Bua, a sea-going luxury yacht that becomes a bunk and breakfast.

DOCKSIDE INN

Boat & breakfast

Imagine awakening in the morning to find your bed undulating ever so gently beneath you. Is it a waterbed? Is it another California earthquake? No, it's only your yacht floating peacefully in the water. You roll over, knowing that breakfast will be taken care of and brought to you shortly.

A growing trend along the California coast, the Dockside Inn is one of several "boat and breakfast" organizations that are providing a unique twist to the traditional bed and breakfast concept—accommodations on a luxury yacht, with breakfast delivered in the morning.

The Dockside Inn is situated in the Harbor Island Marina of San Diego, a short drive from the airport. You check in at an office in the marina, where the "boatkeepers," either Gayle Chrisman or Steve Smith, will greet you and show you to your yacht. For the past year since they opened, Gayle and Steve have recruited a dozen or so private yachts, both power and sail, ranging from 32 to 72 feet. The two partners live on their own sailboat right in

Left, above. The marinascape from the top deck lounge. Below. The interior.

the same marina. ("A short commute," laughs Gayle.)

Although each yacht is a different size, style and configuration, every one is outfitted with modern amenities—a main salon with TV, VCR and stereo; a galley with refrigerator and microwave, and ample sleeping quarters (some holding up to seven guests). No tiny cubicles, the "heads" on several yachts are big enough for a shower-tub. In the morning, guests make their own coffee, and then a continental breakfast-in-a-basket is delivered to their "door".

Within the marina complex are several good seafood establishments, including two Karaoke restaurants, plus a pool that guests can use. A short stroll across Harbor Island Drive provides a picture-perfect view of San Diego Bay and downtown.

DOCKSIDE INN, 2040 Harbor Island Drive, Suite 118, San Diego, CA 92101; (619) 296-8940; (800) 640-RELAX; Gayle Chrisman and Steve Smith, owners. Open all year. Twelve to fifteen luxury yachts, both power and sail, with full heads and showers on board. Rates: $150 to $250, double occupancy, including continental breakfast. Children accepted; no pets; no smoking; Visa/MasterCard. Not all the boats can leave the marina, but sailing and bay charters, whale watching in season, and dive expeditions can be arranged. Waterfront Cafe, Tom Ham's Lighthouse, and Boathouse Restaurant recommended for dining.

DIRECTIONS: from I-5 south, take Airport-Sassafras exit. Follow the signs to the airport (via Kettner and Laurel Streets) and take the East Terminal-Harbor Island exit. Follow the signs to Harbor Island, turn right on Harbor Island Drive, and continue to the Harbor Island West Marina. Check-in office is downstairs next to the Boathouse Restaurant.

KEATING HOUSE

One of San Diego's "Painted Ladies"

When millionaire businessman George Keating came to California in 1886, he was convinced that San Diego had a promising future. He invested heavily in real estate and lived with his family in a Queen Anne Victorian on Banker's Hill just north of the booming downtown.

Today the Keating House stands as a rare reminder of San Diego's bygone Victorian days—rare in a city that is better known for its modern hotels and sunny, lively beaches. With a salmon-and-green exterior and white-trimmed porch, the inn features a multi-gabled roof, octagonal window turret, and fish scale shingles. Canadian and American flags (the Canadian representing owner Larry Vlassoff's Toronto home) now fly from the front, adding to its colorfulness. A garden wraps around the house from the back patio, where jasmine, orchids, roses, and five different varieties of bougainvillea bloom profusely.

In the main house, the front parlor and two floors of bedrooms are filled with comfortable antiques, stained glass, and claw-foot tubs in the shared bathrooms. Each guest room in the main house has been painted in a bright, cheerful color ("We're trying to avoid that dark Adams Family feeling here," says innkeeper Ruth Babb), except for the Music Room, which has retained its original wall-stenciling and a working fireplace. A separate cottage by the garden contains the former butler and chauffeur's bedrooms, each with private bath.

A full breakfast, served in a common dining room, ranges from blueberry pancakes with fresh fruit, to fresh broccoli quiche, to eggs Benedict. All the dishes are garnished with colorful bougainvillea from the garden.

The Keating House is just minutes from San Diego's historic downtown Gaslamp Quarter, where walking tours are conducted through the restored nineteenth-century buildings and shops.

KEATING HOUSE, 2331 2nd Ave., San Diego, CA 92101; (619) 239-8585; Ruth Babb, innkeeper. Open all year. Two rooms in cottage with private baths, 6 rooms in house sharing 3 baths. Rates: $60 to $80 double, including full breakfast. Children welcome; no pets; smoking outside only; Visa/MasterCard/American Express. Fine restaurants within walking distance serving homestyle, California, Mandarin, French, Italian, Russian, Lebanese cuisine. Much to do in San Diego—Balboa Park museums and zoo, Sea World, Old Town restoration, Seaport Village, historic Gaslamp District, ballooning.

DIRECTIONS: from I-5 south exit at Sassafras St. and continue to second traffic light, turning left on Laurel St.; turn right on 2nd Ave. and drive 1½ blocks to inn.

SAN FRANCISCO

VICTORIAN INN ON THE PARK

A superb location

Directly across from the verdant expanse of Golden Gate Park, the Victorian Inn on the Park best evokes turn-of-the-century San Francisco. Innkeepers Lisa and William Benau's splendid Queen Anne-style inn was built in Queen Victoria's diamond jubilee year, 1897, and it supports one of the last remaining belvedere towers in the city.

The interior décor, courtesy of Lisa's mother, Shirley Weber, has an authentic nineteenth-century feel, with velvet bedspreads, William Morris wallpaper, and love seats. The Clunie Room, in shades of light blue and burgundy, is one of the most popular guest rooms, with a gas fireplace and Victorian-style bath. From the Belvedere Room, French doors open to a third-floor balustraded porch within the open belvedere tower that overlooks the park. Behind another set of stained-glass doors is a spacious, tiled, shower-tub. The Redwood Room, with its warm paneling and working fireplace framed by original tiles, is another favorite.

With advance notice, Lisa and Bill will present

a chilled bottle of champagne to their newly arrived guests. For the business traveler, the library is equipped with a large desk, and meetings or business luncheons are easily accommodated.

VICTORIAN INN ON THE PARK, 301 Lyon Street, San Francisco, CA 94117; (415) 931-1830; (800) 435-1967; FAX (415) 931-1830; Lisa and William Benau, hosts. Twelve rooms, each with private bath. Rates: $94 to $154. Includes continental breakfast of fresh fruits and cheese, baked breads, and croissants. Children welcome; no pets; smoking is allowed with consideration to the preferences of other guests; all major credit cards accepted.

DIRECTIONS: from US-101 north, exit at Fell Street and proceed on Fell approximately 9/10ths of a mile to Lyon Street. From US-101 south, exit at 19th Avenue. Turn right on Cabrillo Street, left on 14th Avenue, left on Fulton Street, and right on Lyon Street. Inn is at the corner of Fell and Lyon Streets.

A guest room.

JOHN SWAIN

Left. Washington Square and the cathedral, which the front guest rooms of the inn overlook.

WASHINGTON SQUARE INN

Surrounded by great restaurants

Situated in San Francisco's colorful North Beach, the Washington Square Inn is a perfect place to unwind after a day of city business or sightseeing. A generous afternoon tea of crisp cucumber sandwiches, smoked salmon rolls, cheese, pâté, crackers, wine, and other refreshments awaits guests in the comfortable lobby. In colder weather, you can sink into down-filled couches and warm your feet before a crackling fireplace.

The Washington Square Inn is decorated in understated elegance by designer Nan Rosenblatt, who has owned the inn with her husband, Norm, for nearly fifteen years. Guest rooms are painted in soft pastel colors and furnished with English and French antiques, floral curtains, bedspreads, and paintings. Rooms 7 and 8, both with large bay windows facing the park and its lovely cathedral, have long, inviting window seats.

The inn's friendly staff provides the extras of a small hotel such as valet parking, baggage carried to your room, terry robes, generous fruit baskets, and evening turn-down service with chocolates placed on the pillow. Breakfast can be enjoyed in bed or at the breakfast table in the downstairs lobby.

Washington Square is in the heart of a wonderful Italian-Chinese neighborhood where some of the best restaurants in San Francisco can be found. If the smell of roasting coffee doesn't draw you into a nearby café, then the heady aroma of garlic surely will. Chinatown is a short stroll away, Coit Tower is around the corner, and you can easily catch the cable car to Union Square or Fisherman's Wharf.

In the morning you will arise to find hundreds of Chinese people practicing their *t'ai chi* exercises in the park—a memorable, mesmerizing sight. If you are tempted to join them, go ahead—many of the inn's bolder guests have been known to do just that!

One of the guest rooms.

WASHINGTON SQUARE INN, 1660 Stockton Street, San Francisco, CA 94133; (800) 388-0220, (415) 981-4220 FAX (415) 397-7242; Nan and Norm Rosenblatt, owners; Brooks Bayly, manager. Open all year. Fifteen rooms; 11 with private baths, 4 with shared baths. Rates: $85 to $180, including continental breakfast and afternoon tea. Children accepted; no pets; inn is entirely non-smoking; Visa/MasterCard/American Express/Diners/JCB. Valet parking for extra charge. Buca Giovanni, Amelio's, and Moose's recommended for dining.

DIRECTIONS: from US-101, take Van Ness Avenue north to Union Street and turn right. Turn left on Stockton Street at Washington Square.

The inn consists of two houses on the square.

ALAMO SQUARE INN

A grand era revived

Wayne Corn, who was raised in South Carolina, and Klaus May, a native of Germany's Rhineland, make this the pleasant place it is. Innkeeper Wayne's brand of southern hospitality and resident-chef Klaus's European-style breakfasts herald the revival of that elegant era when continental-style accommodations and gracious service were common-place.

The inn consists of two houses. One is an 1895 blend of Queen Anne and Neo-Classical Revival. A grand split staircase with hand-carved balusters, a stained-glass skylight, formal dining room, and large parlors hark back to an era when luxurious space was fashionable. Wainscoting, rich oak floors, and elegant furnishings blend with an eclectic collection of treasures from Afghanistan, India, Iran, and China.

The adjacent home is an 1896 Tudor Revival. Its simple, cozy parlor has a classic California Craftsman look, featuring original redwood paneling accented by exposed butterfly joinery. Among the upstairs guest rooms, the Art Deco-style Sunrise Suite, with its sunken Jacuzzi, is popular with honeymooners. Guests can find sweeping city views from the third floor balcony of the house.

Connecting the two homes is a partially-covered solarium. Filled with lush ferns and latticework, the solarium is the setting for breakfasts and wedding receptions catered by the innkeepers.

ALAMO SQUARE INN, 719 Scott Street, San Francisco, CA 94117; (415) 922-2055; (800) 345-9888; FAX (415) 931-1304; Wayne Morris Corn, host; Klaus May, resident chef. Thirteen rooms, all with private baths, decorated in period pieces with oriental influence. Rates: $85 to $275. Includes hearty breakfast of omelets, breads, fruits, and fresh-squeezed orange juice. Special dinners, weddings, and conferences by arrangement. Children welcome; no pets; smoking in the solarium only; Visa/MasterCard/American Express.

DIRECTIONS: located on the west side of Alamo Square, ten blocks west of the Civic Center and two blocks north of Fell Street.

Owners Marily and Robert Kavanaugh,
the originators of bed and breakfast in San Francisco.

THE BED & BREAKFAST INN

British charm

Driving along Union Street, it's easy to miss Charlton Court, a narrow cul-de-sac where The Bed and Breakfast Inn is tucked away. Once found, it is like entering a South Kensington mews—a cluster of connecting Victorian buildings with white trim and red geraniums in the window boxes.

This was San Francisco's first bed and breakfast, and is still owned by Robert and Marily Kavanaugh, pioneers of the small city inn. Nearly twenty years ago they found a winning formula—a caring staff, intimate surroundings, and British-style charm—which has resulted in a steady, long-time following.

Four bedrooms with shared baths occupy the Main House, as well as a penthouse flat. Next door, at Two Charlton, are five attractive rooms with private baths. In a third building across the mews is the large Garden Suite, which boasts two bedrooms and baths, a living room and den, greenhouse and private garden.

Guests love the way the inn is safely set back from the noise of the city, but is still so close to the trendy boutiques and cafés of Union Street. It's tempting to leave your car in a nearby garage and walk everywhere from here. The cable cars are less than eight blocks away.

THE BED AND BREAKFAST INN, Four Charlton Court, San Francisco CA 94123; (415) 921-9784; Robert and Marily Kavanaugh, owners. Frankie Stone, manager. Open all year. Two suites with private baths and 9 guest rooms, 5 with private baths and 4 sharing 3 baths. Rates: $70 to $250, including continental breakfast. Children not encouraged; no pets; smoking permitted; French and Spanish spoken; no credit cards; personal checks accepted. Bonta and Pane e Vino recommended for dining nearby.

DIRECTIONS: from US-101 north, take Van Ness Avenue to Union Street and turn left; turn left again on Charlton Court. From US-101 south, exit at Lombard Street. Turn right on Buchanan Street, left on Union Street, and right on Charlton Court.

The Queen Anne Room.

SPENCER HOUSE

A jewel on display

The Spencer House is a well-kept secret in the heart of San Francisco's free-spirited Haight-Ashbury district, of 1960s hippie fame. There is no identifying sign outside, the owners do not have brochures, their phone number is unlisted, and they do not advertise. After seeing the inside of this fabulous Queen Anne mansion, you will agree that there is no need to—word of mouth is enough.

Barbara and Jack Chambers spent two years carefully refurbishing the exquisite 1887 house, which had been run down by neglect. Traveling to England and France, they garnered some of the finest fabrics and antiques to be found at any inn. In the corner of the carved oak foyer stands a lovely grandfather clock, of which only one other exists. Stained glass, 18th and 19th century portraits, inlaid wood floors, sterling silver displays, and overstuffed velvet couches all make this feel like a European house that you would pay to tour. You could be in a Loire Valley chateau.

The six upstairs guest rooms have handsome private baths, and are splendidly decorated with Persian rugs, padded wall coverings, chintz and lace curtains, elaborately-carved headboards, and original Vaseline globe light fixtures. The inviting feather beds have plump, fluffy mattresses, comforters, and pillows you can literally sink into.

Guests are often lured into the huge kitchen, a "must-see", with its scads of copper pots hanging from the ceiling, by the scent of freshly-made coffee cakes and pies. Breakfast is a formal, three to four course, candle-lit affair, served at a long dining room table that is elegantly set with sterling silver and white linen.

SPENCER HOUSE, 1080 Haight Street, San Francisco, CA 94117; (415) 626-9205; Barbara Chambers, owner. Open all year. Six rooms with private baths and double, queen, or king beds. Rates: $95 to $155, including full breakfast. No pets (as two dogs, one cat, and a macaw parrot already reside at the inn); no smoking; Visa/MasterCard to reserve rooms, cash or personal checks in payment.

DIRECTIONS: from US 101 north, exit at Fell Street. After 1 mile, turn left on Baker Street. The inn is on the left at the corner of Baker and Haight Streets.

WILL FALLER

ARCHBISHOP'S MANSION

Where bed and breakfast achieves eminence

Quite simply, this is the most spectacular place to stay in San Francisco. Built for the archbishop of San Francisco in 1904, it survives today for the pleasure of its guests. The original three-story open staircase, with carved mahogany columns, soars upward to a sixteen-foot stained-glass dome. The expansive entry, hallways, and large rooms are characteristic of the Second French Empire style and suggest a grand country manor. Magnificently carved mantelpieces adorn eighteen fireplaces throughout the house, and high arched windows reflect the grandeur of its era.

Whatever has frayed with the passage of time has been restored with integrity. The resplendent painted ceiling in the parlor is fashioned after the decorative detail of a nineteenth-century Aubusson carpet. A palatial environment is created by the blending of Belle Epoque furnishings with Victorian and Louis XIV statuary, paintings, and bronze chandeliers.

Because the city opera house is only six blocks away, all of the guest rooms are named after romantic operas such as Madame Butterfly, La Traviata, and Romeo and Juliet. The Don Giovanni Suite, with its grand parlor and imposing French bed, overlooks the lawns of Alamo Square. The Carmen Room is favored for its luxurious bath—a claw-foot tub which stands in front of a carved wood fireplace. La Tosca is loved for its romantic ambience.

For guests attending concerts at the Davis Symphony Hall or opera house, limousine service for special evenings is provided.

A continental breakfast is brought to your room, and the evening wine hour is accompanied by a Bechstein player piano which was once owned by Noel Coward.

THE ARCHBISHOP'S MANSION, 1000 Fulton Street, San Francisco, CA 94117; (800) 543-5820; (415) 563-7872; Kathleen Austin, manager. Open all year. Fifteen rooms, all with private baths. Eleven rooms have fireplaces, several are full suites with sitting rooms. Rates: $115 to $350, including expanded continental breakfast and wine hour. Children accepted; no pets; smoking is restricted to private rooms only; Visa/MasterCard/American Express. Off-street parking for eight cars and easy street parking. The public rooms are available to guests for cocktail parties, conferences and weddings; catering service.

DIRECTIONS: on northeast corner of Alamo Square at Steiner and Fulton. Alamo Square is 8 blocks west of the Civic Center and 3 blocks north of Fell Street.

SANTA FE

Room #5.

Owner Carolyn Lee.

ALEXANDER'S INN

Utterly charming

It is impossible to avoid using the word "charming" to describe Alexander's Inn. It just slips out of your mouth when you walk through the door.

The red brick foundation and brown shingled roof of this 1903 country cottage are uncommon sights in adobe-filled Santa Fe. Lilac trees frame the entry and envelop the house in a sweet springtime perfume. Inside, these and other colorful flowers are everywhere, contrasting nicely against the cottage white and periwinkle-trimmed walls.

Battenberg lace pillows, Dhurrie rugs, and light wood floors further enhance the fresh, inviting look of the interior. Sunlight streams through a plant-filled common room, where there are rustic wicker chairs, a wood stove, and freshly baked cookies or chips and salsa on the table. Out back is a wooden deck and lawn shaded by more lilacs, wisteria, and apricot trees.

Room Number Five, downstairs, is one favorite, with its four-poster bed, fireplace, stained-glass window, loveseat, and claw-foot tub. Up a narrow flight of stairs are three cozy, romantic bedrooms that feature angled ceilings, dormer windows, and Laura Ashley touches. A separate adobe house behind the inn contains a newly added spacious suite.

Breakfast, taken out on the deck in nice weather, is an ample continental buffet of homemade breads or muffins, homemade granola, yogurt, fresh fruit, juice, and freshly ground coffee.

Owner Carolyn Lee (the inn is named after her son) is a young, easygoing innkeeper who encourages you to feel at home.

ALEXANDER'S INN, 529 East Palace Avenue, Santa Fe, NM 87501; (505) 986-1431; Carolyn Lee, owner; Caroline Cheney, manager. Open all year. Six rooms: 4 with private baths, 2 with shared bath; 2 rooms with fireplaces, and a cottage. Rates: $65 to $150; extra person $15; includes continental plus breakfast and afternoon refreshments. Complimentary bicycles and guest membership at health club provided. Children over 6 accepted; no smoking; French spoken. Visa/MasterCard. Theater, dance, skiing, river rafting, and golf nearby.

DIRECTIONS: From I-25, exit at Old Pecos Trail, which turns into Old Santa Fe Trail. Turn right on Paseo de Peralta, then right on Palace Ave. Inn is 2 blocks up on left.

Owners Louise Stewart and Pat Walter.

GRANT CORNER INN

Breakfast delights

After ordering her breakfast, the guest leaned toward her companion and said, excitedly, "I can hardly wait. . .I remember breakfast so clearly from the last time I was here."

Judging from the subsequent breakfast—apple corn-meal pancakes, bacon, fresh fruit frappés, and three kinds of muffins (chocolate chip, coconut lemon, and carrot)—these types of comments must be heard often at the Grant Corner Inn. Open to the public for weekend brunches, the inn received so many requests for recipes that they published a very successful cookbook.

Breakfast is one of many reasons why Grant Corner Inn is so well known in the Southwest. Situated only two blocks from Santa Fe's downtown plaza, it is conveniently located. Visitors frequently pass by the white picket fence and stop to look at the three-story 1905 colonial house, its gables veiled by delicate shade trees. A wrap-around porch and vine-covered gazebo at the entry add to its appeal.

The interior is mostly American Victorian, with an abundance of antiques, brass and four-poster beds, patchwork quilts, and ceiling fans in the bedrooms. Guests get acquainted over wine and cheese and crackers in the downstairs Wedgewood-blue parlor and dining room.

Grant Corner Inn is also a safe bet for people who want to try an old-fashioned bed and breakfast without losing the professional feel of a hotel. Owner Louise Stewart has a hotel business background (she grew up at the Camelback Inn in Scottsdale, built by her father) that is evident throughout the inn, from the smooth graciousness of her staff to the little amenities—personalized soaps, chocolates on the pillows, fruit baskets, welcome notes, TVs, and phones. She and her husband, Pat Walter (who is usually found in the kitchen whipping up breakfast) have been operating the inn since 1982.

GRANT CORNER INN, 122 Grant Avenue, Santa Fe, NM 87501; (505) 983-6678; Louise Stewart and Pat Walter, owners. Open all year. Thirteen rooms, including a separate 2-bedroom townhouse. Nine rooms with private baths; 4 rooms with 2 shared baths. Rates: $60 to $140, including full breakfast and afternoon wine and cheese. Children over 7 accepted; no pets; smoking on porch only; Spanish spoken. Visa/MasterCard. Museum of Fine Arts, Palace of the Governors, Santa Fe Plaza, shops, and galleries nearby.

DIRECTIONS: From I-25, exit at St. Francis St. and drive north for 3 miles. Turn right on Alameda and drive west 6 miles. Turn left on Guadalupe, then right on Johnson. Inn is 1 mile down on corner of Johnson and Grant.

Breakfast of apple-cornmeal pancakes is served on the porch.

The lap pool.

DOS CASAS VIEJAS

Classic Santa Fe

Dos Casas Viejas, which means "two old houses," embodies classic Santa Fe—the old Southwest blended with touches of modern-day sophistication.

Inside the one-half-acre walled compound are two adobe buildings dating back to 1860. The first, with its original portal, viga ceilings, and Mexican tiled floors, houses a long common area that stretches from the lobby all the way outside to a forty-foot lap pool. The second adobe contains three differently-sized guest accommodations, each with its own private entrance, bricked patio, and kiva fireplace.

The interior is strikingly decorated with bold red accents everywhere. Against the rich flesh tones of the adobe walls in the common room are black and white cowhide chairs and vermilion sofas. Outside are red chile ristras and red geraniums. In one suite are luscious overtones of red; even red bathroom tiles. But for all the red, it is not overdone; rather, it enhances the luxurious feel of the inn.

Owner Jois (who is, not surprisingly, an interior decorator) and Irving Belfield had luxury in mind when they restored and opened Dos Casas Viejas in 1990. The guest quarters are furnished with real Southwest antiques and artwork, down comforters and pillows (and hard-ironed sheets, no less), TVs, and telephones. And, says Jois, "We went out for the softest, thickest towels we could find." Arriving guests enjoy a glass of welcome wine and bowls of chile-flavored pistachios.

DOS CASAS VIEJAS, 610 Agua Fria Street, Santa Fe, NM 87501; (505) 983-1636; Irving and Jois Belfield, owners. Open all year. Five rooms, including 1 suite and 2 mini-suites, all with private baths and fireplaces. Rates: $125 to $185, including welcome refreshments and deluxe continental breakfast. Lap pool on premises. Children not encouraged; no pets; no smoking. Visa/MasterCard. Escalera, Santacafe, and Julian's recommended for dining. Folk Art Museum and galleries nearby.

DIRECTIONS: From I-25, exit at St. Francis Blvd. Drive 3.8 miles north to Agua Fria St. and turn right. Inn is 2 blocks up.

EL PARADERO

A welcoming atmosphere

Built in the early 1800s and representing a mix of Spanish, Territorial, and Victorian eras, this former farmhouse in Santa Fe holds a great deal of architectural interest. Thom Allen and Ouida MacGregor (Ouida is an architect and planner) performed a loving renovation on the structure. The walls, for instance, were restored with a mixture of buttermilk and sand, which gives the surface a nice grainy texture that changes color throughout the day.

But it's the welcoming atmosphere of El Paradero—meaning "stopping place"—that makes a stay here most memorable. A warm living room, breakfast room, and flowery patio provide ample gathering areas. Thom, Ouida, and their staff are friendly and unpretentious, greeting their guests with cider, tea, and snacks in the afternoon. And their abundance of resident pets—two dogs and a cat—are in droll attendance. Ouida says that Mr. Big, their cat, will gladly stay over with guests, and, she adds, with a twinkle in her eye, "He particularly likes to sleep with women."

Ten comfortable Southwest-style guest rooms, some with fireplaces, are in the main building. The most luxurious rooms are upstairs, featuring saltillo tiled floors and tiled baths. Two more Victorian-style suites are found down the block in a separate cottage.

A full breakfast is served in a skylit room amid hanging ferns. The menu includes such unique entrées as *calabasita* frittatas (made with squash, corn, cheese, green chiles, and cilantro) and maple nut muffins, or gingerbread pancakes with lemon sauce, or cinnamon croissant French toast.

Because many people come to Santa Fe nowadays for alternative healing reasons, Ouida says their inn tries to cater to environmentally sensitive products, wool and cotton fabrics, and feather pillows. "Nothing in our inn is artificial."

EL PARADERO, 220 West Manhattan, Santa Fe, NM 87501; (505) 988-1177; Ouida MacGregor and Thom Allen, owners. Open all year. Fourteen rooms, including 2 suites: 10 rooms with private baths, 4 with shared baths; some rooms with fireplaces. Rates: $40 to $130, single; $50 to $130, double, including full breakfast and afternoon refreshments. Children over 4 accepted; pets accepted by arrangement; no smoking; Spanish spoken. No credit cards. Summer opera and chamber music; year-round theatre and arts nearby.

DIRECTIONS: From I-25, take the Old Pecos Trail exit into Santa Fe. Turn left on Paseo de Peralta, then right on Galisteo. Take the first left at Manhattan.

The Piño Suite.

Room No. 6 being visited by Echo, Mr. Bean, and Mr. Big, the inn's resident pets.

SEATTLE

GASLIGHT INN

An exciting blend of old and new

Gaslight Inn was built by Dwight Christianson in 1906, and remained in his family until Trevor Logan and Steve Bennett became owners in 1983. During the process of converting the impressive mansion into a bed and breakfast, Trevor and Steve have maintained its original style while introducing contemporary conveniences.

The home was designed as an example of the various construction features that purchasers could choose from when selecting house plans. The ground floor is a 'four square' design with a grand center hall, two roomy parlors on either side, a library, and a dining room to the rear. Windows feature beautiful beveled glass, while the upstairs landing is illuminated by a decorative stained-glass panel.

A traditional guest room.

Throughout, gleaming oak is fashioned into pillars, paneling, fireplace mantels, and bookcases.

At the turn of the century, when electricity was first introduced, many homes had a combination of gas and electric power. Gaslight Inn retains this unique feature, and derives its name from handsome brass chandeliers with gas flames above glass-shaded lights.

The nine guest rooms are decorated in styles ranging from turn-of-the-century antique, to rustic country and classic contemporary. Much of the midwest oak furniture came from Steve's family, and is typical of items produced for Sears in the early part of this century. The quilts from Trevor's Canadian grandmother go very well with the rich, luster of walnut beds and dressers, or with sleek, modern furnishings. Rooms at the back of the house share wonderful cityscape panoramas of Seattle.

Continental breakfast includes mouth-watering homemade scones and croissants, seasonal fruit, delicious Starbuck's coffee, fresh-squeezed orange juice, and homemade jams, all set out on the sideboard of the elegant oak dining room.

Original Pacific northwest artwork is highlighted, and adds local flavor to most rooms.

GASLIGHT INN, 1727 15th Avenue, Seattle, WA 98122; (206) 325-3654. Trevor Logan and Steve Bennett, innkeepers. Open all year. Two adjoining houses with nine guest rooms, 5 with private baths and 4 shared and 4 with kitchenettes. Rates: $64 to $98, including continental breakfast. Swimming pool; no children; no pets; smoking allowed except in dining room and adjacent parlor; Visa/MasterCard/American Express.

DIRECTIONS: *from the north:* take exit 166 (Denny Way); turn left on Denny; continue to 12th Ave. and turn right; go 1 block and turn left; proceed for 3 blocks turning right onto 15th to '1727' (corner Howell). *From the south:* take the Madison St. exit off I-5; turn right on Madison and continue approximately 15 blocks to 15th Ave.; turn left and go three blocks to corner to '1727' (corner Howell).

KATHERINE JOHNSTON PHOTOS

The swimming pool in the back garden.

The lounge area

M.V. CHALLENGER

An accommodating tugboat

There isn't a more likely place than Seattle to have a bed and breakfast aboard a boat—in this case an ocean-going tug.

Situated on the calm waters of Puget Sound, with its many marinas, docks, wharves, and water frontage, the city is a magnet for sailors of all kinds.

The Motor Vessel Challenger, on the other hand, is a unique haven for armchair sailors who love the sound of lapping water and stars shining in through their porthole window without actually going to sea. (Not that the gleaming machinery below deck isn't ready to go on a moment's notice.)

With eight cabins, all different, there are a variety of accommodations, from single bunks one above the other to the luxurious Master's Cabin, with its private bath, queen-sized bed, private entrance, and windows instead of port holes.

Sea-going life nowadays is much improved over the Challenger's old days as a working tug. A fireplace is the focal point of a sunken conversation pit furnished with overstuffed sofas, and a nearby

working bar is stocked with mixers to suit any drink you can think up. A VCR, with an extensive film library, also helps to while away the time, apart from going ashore and enjoying Seattle's many charms.

The mastermind behind all this is Jerry Brown, from land locked Madison, Wisconsin. Now a confirmed sea dog, he is captain and cook to his guests aboard this wonderfully restored tugboat.

M.V. CHALLENGER, 1001 Fairview Avenue N., Seattle, WA 98109; (206) 340-1201; FAX (206) 621-9201; Jerry Brown, Captain. Open all year. Sleeps 18 in single and double cabins and staterooms, with private baths. Rates: $59.51 to $135.22 single, $81.15 to $135.22 double, including full breakfast. Children by reservation only; no pets; no smoking; Visa/MasterCard/American Express/Diners Club/ Carte Blanche. Situated in the Yale Street Landing area, surrounded by yachts, sloops, houseboats, waterside restaurants, shops, and public parks.

DIRECTIONS: from I-5 take exit 167 and keep to the far right. Stay right at bottom of hill and continue 1 block past Chandler's Restaurant and Cucina Cuchinas and take first left into Yale Street Landing parking lot. With complimentary valet parking. Vessel is located at the far end of the dock.

Left, above. The sea-going tug, the Motor Vessel Challenger. Below. The famous Seattle harborfront market is a cornucopia not to be missed.
FOSTER/ARAKELIAN PHOTO

A stateroom for two.

THE BEECH TREE MANOR

A dynamic woman

Presided over by a colorful and artistic proprietress, Beech Tree Manor offers the traveler modern amenities in a genteel setting. For eight years, Virginia Lucero has held court at this restored turn-of-the-century turquoise mansion on historic Queen Anne Hill amid grounds planted with foxglove, delphinium, roses, and irises.

The interior of the house is dressed in Laura Ashley wallpaper and fabrics, and has an English country house feeling. Original wood, beamed ceilings, and embossed tin walls above the wood paneling in the living room add to the effect.

The emphasis in the dining room is on *food*. Virginia, trained by a Maryland chef, is no slouch in the kitchen. Gourmet breakfasts await guests each morning.

THE BEECH TREE MANOR, 1405 Queen Anne Avenue North, Seattle, WA 98109; (206) 281-7037; Virginia Lucero, owner. Six guest rooms, 3 with private baths, 3 with shared baths. Open all year. Rates: $59 to $79 a couple; $49 to $74 single. Includes a gourmet breakfast. Children over 2 welcome; dogs accepted; smoking restricted; all major credit cards. Walk to Space Needle, opera, ballet, symphony, theater, and restaurants. English bulldog, Chief White Cloud, on premises.

DIRECTIONS: inquire when making reservations.

CHAMBERED NAUTILUS

A stately structure

The Chambered Nautilus is a classic colonial structure situated high on a hill in Seattle's university district. With elegant white columns flanking the entryway and supporting the graceful sun porch, the home is at once stately and gracious.

Both the first-floor living room and adjoining dining room, where innkeepers Bunny and Bill Hagemeyer serve breakfast, are equipped with working fireplaces. Breakfast might include apple quiche, pumpkin-blueberry muffins, or peach muffins prepared by Bunny, who studied with the legendary James Beard. One of Bunny's breakfast recipes was named Recipe of the Year in a national competition among 1500 inns.

Each of the large and airy bedrooms is furnished with thoughtfully coordinated beds and bureaus, and several rooms open onto private porches that overlook the ivy-covered hillside and colorful gardens. Throughout, contemporary graphic prints and delicate watercolors decorate the walls.

After breakfast, visitors may spend the day exploring the pleasures of Seattle and the surrounding area.

CHAMBERED NAUTILUS, 5005 22nd Avenue, N.E., Seattle, WA 98105; (206) 522-2536; Bunny and Bill Hagemeyer, hosts. Six rooms with private and shared baths. Rates: $75 to $97.50 double; single $7.50 less; third person $15; includes full breakfast. Children under twelve by special arrangement; no pets; cigarette smoking on outside porches only; all major credit cards except Discovery. Seminars, business meetings, and receptions can be accommodated. The house is accessible only by a flight of steps.

DIRECTIONS: from I-5, take 50th St. East exit. Proceed about 1½ miles and turn left onto 20th Ave. N.E. Go four blocks and take right onto 54th St. N.E. Proceed down a steep hill and turn right onto 22nd Avenue, N.E.

Breakfast includes "Larry's eggs"—individual soufflés of egg, cheese, cream, and broccoli, perfected by Roberta's son.

ROBERTA'S

Relax
in comfort

Around the turn of the century, Seattle was booming in the wake of the Klondike gold rush. Some of the more affluent families moving to the city began settling in the vicinity of Capitol Hill. Roberta's, a

handsome 1904 residence, is an example of the various roomy and gracious homes that still survive in this house-proud neighborhood.

Roberta's namesake, owner, manager, and innkeeper, Roberta Barry, is a long-time Seattle resident who has been welcoming guests to her bed and breakfast for the past seven years. Exceptionally relaxed, she ensures that everyone enjoys their stay.

The interior of the house is comfortable and uncluttered, with a homey atmosphere. Madrona, Rosewood, Peach, and Plum guest rooms on the second floor feature comfortable queen-sized beds, down comforters, antiques, and locally crafted ceramic sinks in the bathrooms.

ROBERTA'S, 1147 Sixteenth Ave., E., Seattle, WA 98112; (206) 329-3326. Roberta Barry, owner. Open all year. Five guest rooms with queen beds; 4 with private baths and 1 with bath across hall. Rates: $80 to $115, including full breakfast. Children over 12; no pets; no smoking inside; Visa/MasterCard/American Express/Diner's Club. Resident cat, Wally. Seattle Art Museum 1 block.

DIRECTIONS: *from the south:* take exit 166 (Olive Way) off I-5; follow up the hill to 15th Ave. E.; turn left and continue to Prospect; turn right and then left on 16th. *From the north:* take exit 168A (Roanoke) off I-5; turn left at the stoplight and continue to 10th Avenue E.; turn right and follow 10th Ave. E. to E. Boston; turn left and follow until it becomes 15th Ave. E.; turn left on E. Highland and right on 16th Ave. E.

TUCSON

Zelda's Room.

LA POSADA DEL VALLE

Southwest Art Deco

Having opened in 1986, La Posada del Valle set the standard as the first among an ever-growing number of outstanding B&B's in Tucson. From its flowered courtyard to its lovely art deco interior, the inn is, as one guest wrote, "a delightful oasis in the middle of Tucson."

La Posada del Valle, meaning "Inn of the Valley," is a 1929 one-story southwestern home designed by Josias T. Joesler, a renowned Tucson architect. The all-white exterior, large windows, and pastel furnishings give the inn a light, airy feel. Its surrounding courtyard is landscaped with palms, fragrant orange trees, bougainvillea, and colorful spring bulbs.

Owner Debbi Bryant cheerfully greets guests with afternoon tea and homebaked goodies in a long, graceful living room enhanced by understated tones of mauve, grey and salmon, floor-to-ceiling bookshelves, and several striking bronzes (one, the "Winged Victory," signed by Charles Sykes, is the hood ornament for the Rolls-Royce.) Guests are also drawn to the inn's nostalgic 1932 radio.

In keeping with the art deco theme, all five bedrooms are named after a famous woman from the 20s and 30s: Zelda Fitzgerald, Sophie Tucker, Claudette Colbert, Isadora Duncan, and Pola Negri. Some of the bathrooms feature art deco tilework. Sophie's Room boasts an 1818 king-sized bed that once belonged to a fan dancer at Tombstone's Crystal Palace.

Left. *The inn is built around a courtyard.*

Weekday guests (many of whom are visiting the nearby university and medical center) have a continental-plus breakfast—homebaked goods, cereal, fruit, juice, coffee and tea—in the dining room or wicker-filled sun room. On weekends, Debbi and her husband Charles whip up more elaborate dishes, such as cream cheese blintzes with raspberry sauce, or vegetable strudel with parmesan cheese sauce, along with bacon and sausage. Every evening, beds are turned down and a chocolate placed on the pillow.

LA POSADA DEL VALLE BED & BREAKFAST INN, 1640 North Campbell Avenue, Tucson, AZ 85719; (602) 795-3840; Debbi Bryant, owner. Open all year. Five rooms, all with private baths. Rates: $90 to $115, including full breakfast on weekends and continental plus breakfast on weekdays; summer discounts available. Children over 12 preferred; no pets; no smoking; Spanish spoken. Visa/MasterCard. Guest privileges at Tucson Racquet Club included. Arizona-Sonora Desert Museum, Old Tucson Movie Location, and Old Mexico recommended for sightseeing.

DIRECTIONS: From I-10, exit at Grant Rd. Drive east and turn right on Campbell Ave. Turn left on Elm St. and then immediately right into inn's parking lot.

The sitting room.

EL PRESIDIO B&B INN

A jewel

Patti and Jerry Toci spent more than a decade meticulously restoring their 1886 American Territorial home—a unique Victorian adobe in the heart of Tucson's historic El Presidio district. Searching remote villages of Mexico for the right craftsmen and historically authentic materials was, as Patti says, "a task almost too difficult to hurdle." But a walk through this now completed, award-winning jewel leaves no question that their painstaking efforts were handsomely rewarded.

At the center of El Presidio is a traditional Southwestern *zaguán*—an airy, high-ceilinged hall—which Patti has turned into a stunning antiques-filled living room. Off the *zaguán* is The Victorian Suite, with its cheerful parlor, fireplace, white wicker furnishings, and French doors leading out to the garden. In separate tile-roofed buildings off the courtyard are the converted Gate House and Carriage House Suites, both impeccable and beautifully decorated.

Equally impressive are El Presidio's grounds, carved stone fountains, and cobblestoned courtyard. Filled with magnolias, pines, mesquite and fruit trees, lush floral displays, Victorian herbs, and chile *ristras*, this tranquil courtyard is where guests inevitably congregate.

Patti demonstrates a genuine love for her guests that makes even a brief stay a memorable experience in hospitality.

No where is this more evident than at her superb gourmet breakfasts which she presents on fine china and linens in the Veranda Room overlooking the courtyard. Guests are pampered with such sublime pleasures as French toast stuffed with bananas and almond butter, or sweet potato Belgian waffles topped by sautéed apples and yogurt, always accompanied by fresh fruit, bacon, coffee, juice, and a variety of divinely moist muffins.

EL PRESIDIO BED & BREAKFAST INN, 297 North Main Avenue, Tucson, AZ 85701; (602) 623-6151; Patti Toci, owner. Open all year. Four rooms and suites, including a separate carriage house suite; all rooms have private baths; 2 suites have kitchenettes. Rates: $60 to $80, single; $75 to $105 double, including full breakfast and evening refreshments. One child over 12 accepted in Carriage House Suite only; no pets; smoking allowed outside only. No credit cards. Bicycles and guest membership at health club provided. In El Presidio Historic District near arts district and downtown Tucson; museums, restaurants within walking distance.

DIRECTIONS: from I-10, exit at St. Mary's Rd. and drive east. Turn right on Main Ave. Inn is on corner of Main and Franklin.

Owners Val and Mae Robbins

RIMROCK WEST

East meets West

For over twenty years Mae and Val Robbins owned a resort in Pennsylvania called Rimrock East. Then, on a visit to Arizona, they fell in love with the "starkly beautiful expanse of the Southwest." So, they packed away the Poconos for twenty acres in the foothills of northeast Tucson. And, the name of their bed and breakfast hacienda? What else, but Rimrock West!

Rimrock West is a place of real seclusion; an ideal spot to come and paint the dramatic desert scenery and flint-colored mountains. Footpaths meander among the palo verdes, mesquite, and saguaros, where sounds of exotic desert birds are interrupted only by the call of a coyote.

The low-lying, 1960s adobe hacienda with its whimsical, turquoise-painted grillwork is built around a Spanish-style courtyard and trickling fountain. Two bedrooms are on the courtyard, or guests can opt for more privacy in a separate adobe house down by the pool.

Every room is filled with a lifetime of artwork—bronzes, paintings and enamels created by Val, Mae and son Christopher—most of which is for sale.

Breakfast in the courtyard features southwestern eggs with salsa, or corn soufflés, or pancakes, along with vegetable muffins and whipped fresh fruit juice. During the winter, fragrant pecan logs burn twenty-four hours a day in the living room fireplace.

RIMROCK WEST, 3450 North Drake Place, Tucson, AZ 85749; (602) 749-8774; Mae D. Robbins, owner. Open all year. Two rooms and one suite, all with private baths, in main house and 1 adobe guest house. Rates: $85 to $115, including full breakfast; extra person $20. No children; no pets; no smoking; some Spanish spoken. No credit cards. Jerome's, Olive Tree, and Solarium recommended for dining. Art studio, swimming pool, hiking, and bird watching on premises. Sabino Canyon, Mt. Lemmon, horseback riding, and golf nearby.

DIRECTIONS: from Tucson Airport, turn right on Valencia Rd. Turn left on Alvernon Way, which becomes Golf Links Rd. Turn left on Wilmot Rd., which turns into Tanque Verde Rd. Turn left on Catalina Hwy., drive one mile, then turn right on Prince Rd. After another mile, turn right on N. Drake Pl. Hacienda is at the end of N. Drake Pl.

A pool is de rigueur *in the Southwest.*

PEPPERTREES B&B INN

English hospitality in the Southwest

This red-brick Victorian home derives its name from two large old peppertrees which dominate the front yard. Their fragrance, plus the surrounding rosemary, jasmine, and orange blossoms envelop the house in a welcoming perfume.

Innkeeper Marjorie Martin, originally from the Cotswolds, combines English hospitality with a taste of the Southwest at Peppertrees. While her home is furnished with family heirlooms from England, two separate guesthouses called Sunrise and Sunset feature a Southwestern motif. Afternoon tea is highlighted by scrumptious old-fashioned shortbread, while at breakfast guests might feast on blue corn pancakes or Mexican cornbread with turkey sausage.

Both two-story guesthouses offer spacious quarters— each with two bedrooms, full kitchens, living rooms, washers and dryers—off a flowered-filled courtyard with a stone fountain. The Veranda Room, in the main house, has a lovely, more delicate feel. Light streams through an abundance of windows onto a white wrought-iron bed, romantic floral spread, bedside table covered with Battenburg lace and fragrant flowers.

With three professional chefs in Marjorie's family, food is underscored at Peppertrees. As she says, "If you send people away with a full and happy tummy, they're going to remember you." Out of response to guest requests for her recipes, Marjorie wrote her own cookbook which has already sold out its first printing. Her recipes reflect the style of Peppertrees—Southwest flavors (such as chorizo balls and tortilla pancakes) with an English accent. The inn's thriving orange and lemon trees provide fresh ingredients for Marjorie's homemade jams and syrups—another Peppertrees specialty.

PEPPERTREES B&B INN, 724 East University Boulevard, Tucson, AZ 85719; (800) 348-5763; (602) 622-7167; Marjorie G. Martin, owner. Open all year. Ten rooms, 5 with private baths, 5 sharing. Rates: $68 to $140 in winter; $58 to $110 in summer; includes full breakfast and afternoon tea. Children accepted with limitations; smoking allowed on patio only; no pets; French and Spanish spoken. Visa/MasterCard. Delectables, Café Sweetwater, Caruso's, and Café Tierra Cotta recommended for dining. University of Arizona and Arizona State Museum nearby.

DIRECTIONS: from I-10, exit at Speedway and drive east toward University of Arizona. Turn right on Stone Ave., then left on University Blvd. Inn is 7 blocks down University Blvd. on right.

WASHINGTON, D.C.

KALORAMA GUEST HOUSE

A cosmopolitan clientele from around the world

Hidden away from the bustle of the city on a quiet residential street, the Kalorama Guest House is a home away from home. Its thirty-one well appointed rooms are put together with a cozy mix of fine antiques and grandmother's attic that includes beautiful Victorian bedsteads, armoires, and old Singer sewing machines that have been converted to tables.

PHOTOGRAPHS BY MICHAEL ACH

Wrought iron park benches serve as seating for breakfast in the brick-walled dining room.

Vintage photographs, old advertising prints, and portraits decorate the walls, and vases of fresh flowers lend fragrance and color to the public rooms. A generous continental breakfast is served in the brick-walled dining room where wrought iron park benches beside marble top tables afford guests from around the world the opportunity to meet and converse. Friendships can be furthered sipping afternoon sherry before a crackling fire.

Holidays are taken seriously here with a party at Halloween, stockings hung in guest rooms at Christmas, and baskets delivered to all at Easter. The fun-loving staff is attentive, friendly, and always ready to help with directions for sightseeing or museum going. Located in the Adams Morgan section, a vibrant neighborhood of old townhouses, antiques shops, and ethnic restaurants, the Kalorama is a five-minute taxi ride from downtown and all that Washington has to offer.

Noteworthy architectural details highlight a substantial old building.

THE KALORAMA GUEST HOUSE at Kalorama Park, 1854 Mintwood Place, N.W., Washington, DC 20009; (202) 667-6369; Rick Fenstemaker, gen'l mgr., Tamara Wood, host. Open all year. Thirty-one rooms, some with private baths. Rates: $40 to $95, with full continental breakfast and afternoon sherry. There are no provisions for small children; no pets; checks, major credit cards accepted; limited smoking. Limited parking space may be reserved in advance for $5 per night. Over 50 ethnic restaurants to choose from in a 2 block radius.

DIRECTIONS: from Baltimore south on I-95, take the beltway 495 west toward Silver Spring to exit 33. South on Connecticut Avenue towards Chevy Chase. Pass the zoo entrance in the 3000 block and count 4 stop lights and turn left on Calvert St. Go to 2nd stop light and turn right on Columbia; 2 blocks down turn right on Mintwood.

MORRISON-CLARK

The Capitol's Historic Inn

Once two separate townhouses, this historic site evolved into the Soldiers, Sailors, Marines and Airmen's Club to provide affordable hotel accommodations for servicemen during World War II. First Ladies Mamie Eisenhower and later Jackie Kennedy volunteered time here to help with fundraising for the club's operations.

Morrison-Clark (the names of the two original owners) came into existence in 1987, when renovations were completed under the watchful eye of William Adair, who had supervised renovations at the White House. He made certain distinctive features were preserved: the Chinese Chippendale porch, the Shanghai roof, four original pier mirrors, and the Italian Carrera marble fireplaces, among other things.

Each of the 54 guest rooms is unique, many showcasing historical details. Original artwork and authentic period furnishings are complemented by custom designed hand-crafted pieces. Many of the rooms have bay windows, some have porches. An

Left. The wonderful old building that has been transformed into a sleek small hotel.

A luxurious guest room.

A carved marble fireplace.

expanded Continental breakfast is served in the Club Room, the original dining room of the Clark House—elegant with its carved marble fireplaces, gilded mirrors and custom designed bar.

You do not have to leave the inn for what Zagat touts is "some of the best contemporary dining in D.C." There is a choice of dining venues here: The Garden Room for gracious dining with its huge floral centerpiece; The Dining Room, an elegant Victorian drawing room, decorated with Chinoiserie; the Courtyard with a fountain and perennial plantings; or the Veranda, the grand front porch.

Morrison-Clark is the sole historic inn in the nation's capitol, and is much appreciated by its guests. One sent this thank you note:

"Everything has been five star. This is a charmingly elegant inn. Thanks for a memorable experience in Washington, D.C."

MORRISON-CLARK, Massachusetts Avenue and Eleventh Street, NW, Washington, DC 20001; (800) 332-7898, (202) 898-1200, FAX (202) 289-8576; Michael Rawson, general manager. Open all year. 54 rooms and suites with private baths. Rates: *weekdays*, $115 to $165 single; $135 to $185 double; *weekends*, $79 to $135 per room; includes continental breakfast. Children welcome; no pets; smoking and non-smoking rooms, no smoking in dining room; all major credit cards. *Guest services include:* exercise room on premises, complimentary newspapers, concierge, valet parking on premises, babysitting, laundry and dry cleaning, complimentary shoe shine, movie rentals. *Business and conference services:* facsimiles and photocopying, secretarial and clerical, notary public.

DIRECTIONS: in the White House area on Massachusetts Avenue, a main thoroughfare.

Some of the art nouveau collection.

LOGAN CIRCLE

Extravagantly restored

Extensively restored by two loving owners, this one-hundred-year-old Victorian mansion features original wood paneling, stained-glass niches, ornate chandeliers, and a Victorian-style lattice porch and gardens. A mecca for lovers of "Art Nouveau," its walls are covered with highly selective and artfully framed posters, prints, magazine covers, and advertising art. The hostess, a tireless collector, is constantly adding new pieces to her collection.

In addition to the house's own beautiful appointments, the owners have incorporated some Victorian gems rescued by architectural salvagers: gilded mirrors, intricately carved mantels, and glistening English tiles. Floral patterns combine with silks, violet walls, wainscoting, draperies, oriental rugs, Eastlake furniture, and vintage floors, creating a romantic ambiance. One of two parlors houses a working player piano with silk-fringed turquoise shawl.

Each of the five guest rooms is singular and charming. An additional ground floor apartment offers complete privacy and comfort. Guest room furnishings include antique quilts, wicker, greenery, shutters, wash bowls, a Jacobean desk, and a four-poster bed.

Overlooking a fountain and rose arbor, the latticed porch seduces with a promise to banish worldly cares. Here one can effortlessly return to the romance and elegance of by-gone days.

LOGAN CIRCLE. Six guest rooms with shared baths and 1 apartment with private bath. Open all year. Rates: $60 to $70 single, $70 to $80 double; apartment $75 single, $85 double; continental breakfast included. Children welcome; no pets; no smoking. *Represented by Bed & Breakfast Accommodations Ltd.*, P.O. Box 12011, Washington, DC 20005; (202) 328-3510, FAX (202) 332-3885; Visa/MasterCard/American Express.

DIRECTIONS: given on reservation.

B & B RESERVATION AGENCIES

ATLANTA

BED & BREAKFAST ATLANTA, 1801 Piedmont Avenue, Suite 208, Atlanta, GA 30324; (800) 967-3224, (404) 875-0525, FAX (404) 875-9672; Madalyne Eplan and Paula Gris. 9:00 A.M. to 12:00 P.M. and 2:00 P.M. to 5:00 P.M. Monday to Friday. *Accommodations in the city's most desirable "close-in" neighborhoods. Charm, comfort, convenience; Kosher arrangements available.* Handling homestay accommodations for 1996 Olympics.

R.S.V.P GRITS, 541 Londonberry Road NW, Atlanta, GA 30327; (800) 823-7787, (404) 843-3933, FAX (404) 252-8886; Marty Barnes. 9 A.M. to 6 P.M. Monday to Friday. *Bed and breakfast inns and homestays in Atlanta and within a 100 mile radius. 1996 Olympic reservations.*

BALTIMORE

AMANDA'S BED & BREAKFAST RESERVATION SERVICE, 1428 Park Avenue, Baltimore, MD 21217; (800) 899-7533, (410) 225-0001, FAX (410) 728-8957; Betsy Grater. 9:00 A.M. to 5:00 P.M. weekdays. *Private homes, yachts and small inns in Baltimore, Maryland, and nearby states.*

THE TRAVELLER IN MARYLAND, P.O. Box 2277, Annapolis, MD 21404; (410) 269-6232; Greg Page. 9 A.M. to 5 P.M. Monday to Friday. *Yachts, inns, private homes.*

BOSTON

BED AND BREAKFAST ASSOCIATES, Bay Colony, Ltd., P.O. Box 57166, Babson Park Branch, Boston, MA 02157-0166; (617) 449-5302, FAX (617) 449-5958; Arline Kardasis, Marilyn Mitchell. Monday to Friday 9 A.M. to 5 P.M. *Eastern Massachusetts.*

BED AND BREAKFAST CAMBRIDGE AND GREATER BOSTON, P.O. Box 1344, Cambridge, MA 02238; (800) 888-0178, (617) 576-1492; Pamela Carruthers. 10 A.M. to 6 P.M. Monday–Friday; 10 A.M. to 3 P.M. Saturday. *Private and vacation homes of every description in Boston, Cambridge, and Lexington.*

HOST HOMES OF BOSTON, P.O. Box 117, Waban Branch, Boston, MA 02168; (617) 244-1308, FAX (617) 244-5156; Marcia Whittington. 9 A.M. to 12 noon, 1:30 to 4:30 P.M. *Covers Boston and select city suburbs.*

CHARLESTON

HISTORIC CHARLESTON BED & BREAKFAST, 60 Broad Street, Charleston, SC 29401; (803) 722-6606, FAX (803) 722-9773; Douglas Lee, owner; Pam Strange, manager. 9 A.M. to 5 P.M. Monday to Friday. *Historic properties dating from 1720 to 1890, up-to-date with all modern conveniences. Private homes, carriage houses, and mansions.*

CHICAGO

BED & BREAKFAST/CHICAGO, INC., P.O. Box 14088, Chicago, IL 60614-0088; (312) 951-0085, FAX (312) 649-9243; Mary Shaw. 9 A.M. to 5 P.M. Monday to Friday except Dec., Jan. Feb. 9 A.M. to 1 P.M. *Full range of personalized accommodations in private homes and bed and breakfast inns.*

HERITAGE BED & BREAKFAST REGISTRY, 75 East Wacker Drive, Suite 3600, Chicago, IL 60601; (312) 857-0800, FAX (312) 857-0805; Bill Edlebeck. 9 A.M. to 5 P.M. Monday to Friday, 12 noon to 5 P.M. Saturday. *20 places in Downtown and Old Town areas.*

DALLAS/FORT WORTH

BED & BREAKFAST TEXAS STYLE. 4224 W. Red Bird Lane, Dallas, TX 75237; (214) 298-8586, FAX (214) 298-7118; Ruth Wilson. 8:30 A.M. to 4:30 P.M. Monday to Friday. *Homestays.*

KANSAS CITY

BED & BREAKFAST KANSAS CITY, P.O. Box 14781, Lenexa, KS 66285; (913) 888-3636; Edwina Monroe. *30 places from 1892 Victorian to a Geodesic Dome in the woods.*

LOS ANGELES

BED & BREAKFAST OF LOS ANGELES, 3924 East 14th Street, Long Beach, CA 90804; (800) 383-3513, (310) 498-0552 (also for FAX); Robin Nahin. 7 A.M. to 10 P.M. 7 days a week. *B&Bs, small inns, and homestays.*

EYE OPENERS BED & BREAKFAST RESERVATIONS, Box 694, Altadena, CA 91003; (213) 684-4428 or (818) 797-2055 FAX (818) 798-3640; Ruth Judkins and Elizabeth Cox. 9 A.M. to 6 P.M. *Private homes and bed and breakfast inns in Los Angeles, San Diego, San Francisco, and throughout California.*

MIAMI

BED & BREAKFAST CO., P.O. Box 262, South Miami, FL 33243; (305) 661-3270 [and for Faxes]; Marcella Schaible. 9:00 A.M. to 5:00 P.M. Monday to Friday. *All of Florida including islands off the coast, from an Art Deco mansion on an island in Biscayne Bay to unhosted apartments along the coast.*

NEW ORLEANS

BED & BREAKFAST, INC., 1021 Moss Street, Box 52257, New Orleans, LA 70152-2257; (800) 729-4640, (504) 488-4640, FAX (504) 525-4640; Hazell Boyce. *Deluxe B&B's in lovely and historic locations in New Orleans.*

SOUTHERN COMFORT BED & BREAKFAST RESERVATION SERVICE. P.O. Box 13294, New Orleans, LA 70185; (800) 749-1928, (504) 861-0082, FAX (504) 861-3087. Paula Bandy. 9 A.M. to 1 P.M. Monday to Friday. *Homestays.*

NEW YORK

AT HOME IN NEW YORK, P.O. Box 407, New York, NY 10185; (800) 692-4262, (212) 956-3125, FAX (212) 247-3294; Lois Rooks. 9:30 A.M. to 5:30 P.M. Monday to Friday, 9:30 A.M. to noon Saturday and Sunday. *From artists' lofts to brownstones to high rise accommodations.*

BED AND BREAKFAST (& BOOKS), 35 West 92nd Street, New York, NY 10025; (212) 865-8740; Judith Goldberg. 10 A.M. to 5 P.M. Monday to Friday. *A unique New York City service offering a selection of hosts who work as photographers, psychologists, lawyers, dancers, teachers, and artists, with special knowledge of New York's rich cultural life.*

CITY LIGHTS BED & BREAKFAST LTD., P.O. Box 20355, Cherokee Station, New York, NY 10028; (212) 737-7049, FAX (212) 535-2755; Yedida Nielson. 9:00 A.M. to 5:00 P.M. Monday to Friday; 9:00 A.M. to 12:00 P.M. Saturday. Two night minimum stay. *Hosted and unhosted apartments from studios to four bedrooms in apartment houses and brownstones in Manhattan, Park Slope, Brooklyn Heights, and Queens. Ask about Europe.*

NEW WORLD BED AND BREAKFAST, 150 Fifth Avenue, Suite 711, New York, NY 10011; (800) 443-3800; (212) 675-5600; Kathleen Kruger. 9:30 A.M. to 5 P.M. Monday to Friday. Two night minimum stay. *Hosted and unhosted apartments in high rises, brownstones, and carriage houses in Manhattan.*

URBAN VENTURES, INC., P.O. Box 426, New York, NY 10024; (212) 594-5650, FAX (212) 947-9320; 9 A.M. to 5 P.M. Monday to Friday. Mary McAulay. *Manhattan and other boroughs.*

PHILADELPHIA

BED & BREAKFAST CENTER CITY, 1804 Pine Street, Philadelphia, PA 19103; (800) 354-8401, (215) 735-1137; Bill Buchanan. 9:00 A.M. to 9:00 P.M. seven days. *Represents 50 places from simple to luxurious townhouses in Philadelphia's Center City, Rittenhouse Square, Antique Row, Society Hill, University City, Art Museum area.*

BED & BREAKFAST CONNECTIONS, P.O. Box 21, Devon, PA 19333; (800) 448-3619, (215) 687-3565, FAX (215) 995-9524; Lucy Scribner and Peggy Gregg. 9 A.M. to 7 P.M. Monday to Friday, 9 A.M. to 5 P.M. Saturday. *Everything from historic townhouses to small, charming B&B inns.*

PHOENIX/SCOTTSDALE

ARIZONA ACCOMMODATIONS RESERVATIONS, Gallery 3 Plaza, 3819 North Third Street, Phoenix, AZ 85012; (800) 266-7829, FAX (602) 263-7762. 9 A.M. to 5 P.M. Monday to Friday. *Homestays.*

MI CASA SU CASA B&B ACCOMMODATIONS. P.O. Box 950, Tempe, AZ 85280; (800) 456-0682, (602) 990-0682, FAX (602) 990-3390. Ruth Thomas Young. 8 A.M. to 8 P.M. daily. *Publishes a B&B guide with some pictures.*

PORTLAND

BED & BREAKFAST RESERVATIONS—OREGON, 2321 N.E. 28th Avenue, Portland, OR 97212; (503) 287-4704; Milan Larsen. 9 A.M. to 7 P.M. Monday thru Saturday. *Oregon coast turn-of-the-century architecture to ultra-modern; early 1900's to contemporary homes in Portland; ranches, farms and mountain country accommodations throughout Oregon.*

NORTHWEST BED AND BREAKFAST RESERVATION SERVICE, 610 S.W. Broadway, Suite 606, Portland, OR 97205; (800) 365-6343, (503) 243-7616; LaVonne Miller, owner; 8 A.M. to 8 P.M. 7 days a week. *Farms, ranches, Victorian, contemporary, mountain, and ocean front homes.*

ST. LOUIS

RIVER COUNTRY BED & BREAKFAST RESERVATION SERVICE, 1900 Wyoming Street, St. Louis, MO 63118; (314) 771-1993; Mike McGill-Warner. 10 A.M. to 5 P.M. Monday to Friday.

SAN ANTONIO

BED & BREAKFAST HOSTS OF SAN ANTONIO AND SOUTH TEXAS. Lavern Campbell. 123 Auditorium Circle, San Antonio, TX 78205; (800) 356-1605, (210) 222-8846. 9 A.M. to 5 P.M. Monday to Friday. *Some homestays.*

SAN ANTONIO LODGING LINE, 217 Alamo Plaza, Suite 300, San Antonio, TX 78205; (800) 858-4303, (210) 227-6667; Doug Beach. 8:30 A.M. to 5:30 P.M. Monday to Friday and Saturday 9 A.M. to 6 P.M. in summer.

SAN DIEGO

BED & BREAKFAST GUILD OF SAN DIEGO, P.O. Box 3292, San Diego CA 92163; (800) 266-1400, (619) 523-1300. 9 A.M. to 5 P.M. Monday to Friday.

CAROLYN'S BED & BREAKFAST HOMES, in San Diego, 416 Third Avenue #25, Chula Vista, CA 92010; (619) 422-7009; Carolyn Moellar. 9 A.M. to 6 P.M. San Diego county and Los Angeles area.

SAN FRANCISCO

BED AND BREAKFAST INTERNATIONAL, P.O. Box 282910, San Francisco, CA 94128-2910; (800) 872-4500 (415) 696-1690, Sharene Klein. 8:30 A.M. to 5 P.M. weekdays; 9 A.M. to noon on Saturdays. *Private homes, apartments, houseboats, and inns. California, Las Vegas, and Tahoe.*

BED AND BREAKFAST SAN FRANCISCO, P.O. Box 420009, San Francisco, CA 94142; (800) 452-8249, (415) 931-3083, FAX (415) 921-2273; Susan and Richard Kreibich. Call Monday to Friday 9:30 A.M. to 5 P.M. *Victorians, houseboats, and modern accommodations, all including full breakfast.*

SANTA FE

BED & BREAKFASTS OF NEW MEXICO. P.O. Box 2805, Santa Fe, NM 87504; (505) 982-3332. Rob Bennett. 9 A.M. to 5 P.M. Monday to Friday. *Homestays and Casitas.*

SANTA FE CENTRAL RESERVATIONS, 320 Artist Road, Suite 10, Santa Fe, NM 87501; (800) 776-7669, (505) 983-8200, FAX (505) 984-8682; Alicia Dopson. 8 A.M. to 5 P.M. Monday to Friday.

SEATTLE

PACIFIC BED & BREAKFAST AGENCY, 701 N.W. 60th Street, Seattle, WA 98107; (206) 784-0539, FAX (206) 782-4036; Irmgard Castleberry. 9 A.M. to 5 P.M. weekdays. *Mansions, Victorians, island cottages, and contemporary lakefront homes. Covers all of Washington and British Columbia. Directory available for $5.00.*

A TRAVELLERS' BED & BREAKFAST RESERVATION SERVICE, P.O. Box 492, Mercer Island, WA 98040; (206) 232-2345, FAX (206) 679-4533; Diane Teterud. 10 A.M. to 5 P.M. (winter), 9 A.M. to 5 P.M. (summer), weekdays. *Guest houses, inns, and private residences. Over 200 accommodations in the Pacific Northwest, including Vancouver and Victoria, British Columbia and Oregon coast. Assists in personal itineraries including ferries.*

TUCSON

MI CASA SU CASA B&B ACCOMMODATIONS. P.O. Box 950, Tempe, AZ 85280; (800) 456-0682, (602) 990-0682, FAX (602) 990-3390. Ruth Thomas Young. 8 A.M. to 8 P.M. daily. *Publishes a B&B guide with some pictures.*

WASHINGTON, D.C.

THE BED & BREAKFAST LEAGUE/SWEET DREAMS & TOAST, P.O. Box 9490, Washington, DC 20016; (202) 363-7767; Millie Groobey. 9 A.M. to 5 P.M. Monday to Thursday, 9 A.M. to 1 P.M. Friday. *Washington, D.C. and adjacent suburbs.*

BED 'N' BREAKFAST LTD. OF WASHINGTON, D.C., P.O. Box 12011, Washington, DC 20005; (202) 328-3510, FAX (202) 332-3885; Jackie Reed. 10 A.M. to 5 P.M. weekdays, 10 A.M. to 1 P.M. Saturday. *Washington metropolitan areas, specializing in the historic districts.*